Dear Ros,
You'll ~~love~~ this one, too.

WHEN THE WRONG THING IS RIGHT

It's by a really good friend of ours —

Much Love,
Julie + Tim

WHEN THE WRONG THING IS RIGHT

How To Overcome Conventional Wisdom, Popular Opinion, And All The Lies Your Parents Told You

SYLVIA BIGELSEN, ED.S.
AND VIRGINIA MCCULLOUGH

MASTERMEDIA LIMITED
NEW YORK

© 1994 by Sylvia Bigelsen and Virginia McCullough

All rights reserved, including the right of reproduction, in whole or part, in any form.

Published 1994 by MasterMedia Limited

MASTERMEDIA and colophon are registered trademarks of MasterMedia Limited.

Library of Congress Cataloging-in-Publication Data

Bigelsen, Sylvia.
    When the wrong thing is right : how to overcome conventional wisdom, popular opinion,
and all the lies your parents told you /
Sylvia Bigelsen and Virginia McCullough.
      p. cm.
    ISBN 0-942361-99-7 : $9.95
    1. Conduct of life. 2. Autonomy (Psychology)
3. Self-actualization (Psychology)
I. McCullough, Virginia. II. Title.
BF637.C5B48 1994
158—dc20   94-21412

DEDICATION

For those closest to my heart: my husband, Fred Bigelsen, and our children and their spouses, who have both praised and criticized my "wrong" ideas, but supported me anyway. And to my grandchildren, Brittany, Samantha, and Ryan, whom I hope will grow up secure enough to make their own decisions.

Contents

Introduction xi

ONE   Is The Wrong Thing Always Wrong? 3

TWO   Whose Attitudes Are These Anyway? 15

THREE Learning To Make Choices Your Own Way 35

FOUR Love, Marriage, and Divorce 59

FIVE Sex, Lies, and Affairs 87

SIX Parents, Siblings, and Children 113

SEVEN Money, Careers, and Lifestyles 149

EIGHT Judging "Books" By Their Covers 167

NINE Moving Forward In Your Own Way 181

About the Authors 195

Acknowledgments

Many people helped us bring this book into being. Among them, of course, are my clients, who brought their sorrows and dilemmas, but also their unique ways of viewing their lives. It goes without saying that I learned a lot from them and they have helped shape the ideas presented in this book.

My wonderful children, Stephen, Nancy, Jayne, David, and Faith, also provided encouragement and support. My colleagues and friends, especially Gloria Sloane, generously shared their personal stories and inspired me to keep going. All these individuals showed me that there are at least three sides to every story—and usually many more.

There were also people involved who usually remain behind the scenes. Anne Wyeville played a crucial role, as did our agent Lyle Steele and his midwest project developer, Jim Kepler. Our assistant, Lu Buckmaster of Chicago, Illinois, cheerfully and efficiently met all our deadlines.

I'd also like to thank my coauthor, Virginia McCullough, who made organizing and writing this manuscript so easy. Finally and especially, thanks to my dear husband, Fred Bigelsen, who gave advice, suggestions, and as always, loving support.

Sylvia Bigelsen

INTRODUCTION

Throughout my professional life, I've assumed that people choose to seek help from a counselor because they are experiencing confusion, unhappiness, and difficulty making life-changing decisions. Therefore, the situations my clients found themselves in were not surprising, at least most of the time. But what I did find surprising was the variety of choices my clients made. Many of their decisions were unconventional, went against what they (and I) had been taught was correct or "normal," and didn't always fit within the range of possibilities presented by "experts"—including me.

I also observed how unhappy and dissatisfied many people were, because they believed they were constrained from making a decision that was not conventional. Even though they knew in their hearts what was best for them, they assumed (usually correctly) that these decisions would prompt a chorus of critics. However, I became so impressed by the hard work these clients undertook in order to free themselves from ingrained messages, popular truisms, and value systems that no longer worked, that the idea for this book gradually formed. If my clients could lead happier lives by struggling to make decisions their own way, I concluded, then we can all benefit from their experiences.

I have no doubt that as you read through the issues presented in the following chapters, you may disagree—sometimes strongly—with some of the choices made by the people involved. I've also had my share of reservations. But it is my hope that some of your decisions and attitudes will be affirmed and validated, especially if you have made choices from your heart, only to be ridiculed and criticized later.

Whether I have agreed with my clients' choices or not, I gained a growing respect for their right to make their own decisions in their own way. I have watched these people enjoy the happy results and I also have observed as they took responsibility for choices that didn't turn out so well.

My primary goal for this book is to help you gain the confidence you need to break free from the voices of "well meaning" people and the advice of the "experts." It is possible that the "right" choice you are urged to make may be the "wrong" choice for you.

Because I respect my clients' right to privacy, names and specific circumstances have been changed. Actual names have been used only in obvious situations, such as those involving my immediate family. Early in the writing, a few people heard some of the "stories," and exclaimed, "Hey, that's me." However, we had no knowledge of that person's situation. Such strong identification reinforces the idea that some situations are more common than any of us realize. So, if you find yourself having a strong, even unpleasant, identification, take some comfort in knowing that you are not alone with your problem. And, you may also happily conclude that others share similar pleasures and joys.

When The Wrong Thing Is Right

ONE

Is The Wrong Thing Always Wrong?

The first thing I noticed about John and Laurie was what an attractive couple they were. Both were tall and fashionably dressed—the picture of a chic, successful couple. Laurie and John enjoyed their careers, shared many interests, and had built a satisfying life together, a life they both valued. When I asked them why they had sought marriage counseling, they said they needed to work out problems that were the aftermath of John's affair with a coworker. This affair had ended immediately after Laurie discovered it, and John had spent months begging and pleading for his wife's forgiveness. John described their marriage as "going from rocky to disastrous." But both agreed they were committed to saving their marriage.

John and Laurie made almost no progress during the first eight months of therapy. In fact, I wondered why they continued to come back. The main obstacle seemed to come from Laurie. Although Laurie claimed to still love John very deeply, she just couldn't seem to forgive and forget.

One evening during an otherwise uneventful counseling session, Laurie suddenly blurted, "I just had my own affair." Her arms were folded across her chest and she looked straight at John as she made her announcement. John was horrified—more outraged than either Laurie or I would have expected. However, from that night on, both John and Laurie were able to get down to business and work on their problems. Within a few weeks, they were starting to live happily together again. A few months later they took off on a long vacation and when they returned, they announced that they didn't need my help any longer. They were right about that. Laurie's affair had made a major difference in their lives.

If Laurie had asked me—and she didn't—whether a "get even" affair was a good idea, I probably would have said no, that getting revenge is not advantageous and usually creates more problems than it solves. Most people, therapists included, believe that, except for inflicting physical violence, it's the worst thing the wronged partner can do. But I believe that in this couple's case, Laurie's affair was the breakthrough that ultimately allowed the marriage to be healed. I'm not certain that Laurie ever would have found the capacity to forgive and forget. Furthermore, John was now able to understand Laurie's rage and hurt because he had his own experience of betrayal to deal with. So, regardless of my own professional judgment, Laurie's actions paved the way to saving the marriage.

This was not the first time I'd observed my clients taking actions and making decisions that were contrary to well accepted professional—and conventional—wisdom. It also was not the first time that I'd watched these actions result in a satisfied and happy person going his or her way, unencumbered by nagging voices of convention. Over the years, as I've thought about this, I've come to the conclusion that there are times when the so-called correct decision is just not suitable. In fact, some of the deepest unhappiness I see is often the result of a failure to listen to one's own inner truth, truth that may not be compatible with popular opinion and conventional values.

Part of the struggle so many clients face is the hard decision to follow their own star, make their own choices, and take responsibility for the results. That struggle was only made more difficult when some real or imagined "authority" figure was looking over their shoulder, figuratively speaking, and pushing them to conventional solutions to problems.

A Destructive Myth

I'll never forget how sad Mike became as he agonized about going to medical school. Against his own better judgment he had enrolled in one of the top schools in the country and in spite of hating it, he actually was doing quite well. However, anyone could see that he was miserable. "My parents expect me to finish," he said again and again. "I don't know how I can let them down." Guilt, sheer guilt, was keeping him from following his own dreams.

Frankly, Mike's parents were snobs. They didn't like it one bit that when he was a young child, Mike showed great mechanical ability. They didn't care if he could fix everything from his bike to the toaster; his parents wanted him to be a *professional*—preferably a doctor, but a lawyer at the very least. Mike wanted to enter a field in which his talents could be developed, but his parents and other relatives belittled his desires, and eventually he'd caved in.

Fortunately, after months of deliberation and emotional pain, Mike walked out of medical school and found a temporary job using his mechanical skills. Even though he wasn't well paid, he could support himself while he took the time to explore what he really wanted to do.

To this day, Mike's parents and most of his relatives label him a quitter. Only Mike, a few of his friends, and I know how much courage it took for him to commit the so-called sin of quitting something he'd started. Almost every authority figure in his life had preached that quitters are weak, that they will never finish anything. But I believe it took strength for Mike to go against authoritative and conventional wisdom and get out of something that was wrong for him in the first place. I hope that the family-will eventually come to see that by belittling Mike's choice, they are driving him away.

Once a person has the strength to break free, he or she is changed in many ways. An assertive shift in one part of life often brings changes in other areas. So, the snobbery, the pressure, and the disapproval may move Mike to minimize contact with his family. In short, he'll seek more pleasant and supportive company.

All his life, Mike (and almost everyone else in our society) had been taught this adage: Quitters never win and winners never quit. Karen, a woman in her forties still finishes every book she starts reading, no matter how boring it is. Ray, a man in his thirties, is still trying to learn to play chess even though he appears to have no patience for it. After all, he'd started something, so he's obligated to finish. In these cases, professionals weren't involved—Karen and Ray were labeling themselves quitters.

The notion that we should never quit what we start is one of the truisms, words to live by, and, at least in some cases, a rule we should follow in order to live well—or live "right." Sometimes we simply call this conventional wisdom. Conventional wisdom dictates that Laurie shouldn't have an affair to get even with her husband. Conventional wisdom says that if you have the opportunity to be a doctor you should grab it. Conventional wisdom has a rule for just about every situation we encounter in life, from our sexual behavior to our attitudes about money.

How often do we question these rules? Do we ever say, "Whose idea was that anyway?" All through our lives we absorb these truisms, this conventional wisdom, and we end up with a fairly standard set of choices for any circumstance we find ourselves in. According to popular opinion, there is a finite number of solutions to each problem, and we often believe that we should restrict our thinking to that narrow group of ideas. Yet I, and I'm sure many of my colleagues, hear our clients bring up unconventional options and act in ways that aren't "sanctioned"— and they still end up happy. These clients also may be surprised that there isn't necessarily a big price to pay for acting against authority.

On the other hand, there may be a price for unconventional choices. Mike had to endure humiliating criticism from his family. At some point, it might diminish on its own, or Mike could simply refuse to listen. I've seen many clients inch toward decisions, rather than make them with confidence and ease, because they are afraid of the consequences. Sometimes this timidity makes perfect sense.

Deciding to get a divorce, for example, almost always leads to significant changes in a person's life. It may affect everything from money to children to career choices. Other people might disapprove and even be rejecting. As one of my clients, Betty, put it, "Everyone thinks Frank is so special and dear. They don't see his cruel side, and I know people will think I'm nuts for leaving a man they all consider a real find." Betty searched her soul for more than a year before she followed her heart and left. And Betty was right—her family and friends did think she was being foolish. Frank was rich, Frank was handsome, Frank was witty and entertaining. One of her close friends even aggressively pursued Frank when Betty left him. Six months into the relationship, she left him too. It turned out Frank's cruel side didn't exist just in Betty's imagination.

Even when a person knows a decision is the right thing to do, he or she may agonize for months—even years—before taking that step.

I've seen people go through almost as much agonizing over small choices or changes as they do over major turning points in life. A man who had not had the opportunity to go to college while in his twenties, debated with himself for months over a decision to take some classes at a community college. He felt silly, he said. A man in his late forties shouldn't be starting over. The voice that told him this was a parental one. His parents had always acted as if life was almost over when you turned forty, and what you were at that age set the tone for the years you had left. To break out of that image and change life drastically was to appear unbalanced, and heaven knows, no one wants that. When voices of authority are involved, decisions large and small can be accompanied by fear.

WHERE DOES THIS AUTHORITY COME FROM ANYWAY?

Despite the rapid rise of self-help and personal growth groups, our society still pays an enormous amount of attention to authority figures. Parents, teachers, relatives, ministers, rabbis, priests, friends, relatives, and even our next-door neighbors are ready sources of advice, much of it sound and thoughtful—to a point. And then there are the professionals who offer their advice and counsel one on one and through the worlds of electronic and print media. Therapists from numerous schools of psychology, child development experts, physicians, lawyers, and so on, regularly offer their expertise on everything from toilet training to saving a marriage to placing a parent in a nursing home. Of course, much of the advice we receive from these professionals is reliable and caring. Many of us have been helped in significant ways because we consulted a professional when we were in trouble.

However, during many years of working as a therapist with individuals and couples, I have seen client after client make sound decisions that friends, family, and often other professionals disapproved of. And often, it was the disapproval of others that caused my clients problems and emotional pain, not a decision itself.

Even though I'm a psychotherapist, I am well aware that some of the advice we receive—from professionals and nonprofessionals alike—is based on hosts of truisms and conventional wisdom. Of course, professional psychological advice, generally sought in individual therapy, has the weight of education and training behind it. But this advice can also be restricted to, or molded around certain "correct" attitudes and actions that are widely embraced. Conventional wisdom tells us what is good and bad, wise or foolish, right or wrong, and healthy and unhealthy. The message, subtle or not so subtle, is that deviating from this wisdom will likely lead to disaster. But sometimes the joke is on the authorities giving out this advice. I've been amazed again and again by how happy people can be with their decisions once they are freed from an inflated respect for this advice.

The Case of the Disobedient Kid

We all know that children, especially girls, should be nice to each other. But we also know that this isn't always the case. However, according to conventional wisdom, even when they're not treated well, "nice" children don't retaliate—not ever. A ten-year-old girl I know was relentlessly tormented by other children for being overweight. For years, she was the butt of jokes, but her parents told her that if she just ignored the teasing, it was sure to stop.

One particular girl was the worst of the tormentors. She was a skinny, rather ugly girl who wore glasses, but because she wasn't fat, she was accepted by the other kids. The overweight child finally determined that she would beat up this skinny girl—she'd show her strength and prove that she couldn't be pushed around any longer. She announced her intentions to her parents, hoping they would be pleased by how strong she was being. "No, no," her parents said, "nice girls don't do that." In this family, being nice counted for more than being respected. But one day, when this little girl just couldn't take it any longer, she waited for the mean girl, grabbed her and punched her so hard the girl's glasses broke. Yes, the parents became involved and the overweight girl was punished for disobeying. The glasses were replaced and it was assumed that was the end of the incident.

Because I was that overweight ten-year-old girl, I know that replacing the glasses didn't represent the end of that story. It was an important event for me because, contrary to what I'd been told, the kids did stop teasing me—they even showed me much greater respect. My parents tried to make me feel guilty for what I'd done, but I just couldn't manage that "correct" feeling. In fact, I felt great! Taking revenge may not have been "right," but it sure felt good and it made my life easier.

I'm not sure what would have happened to me if I'd followed the dictums of the authority figures in my life. I do know that this experience planted the seed of questioning both authority and the truisms by which we're supposed to live—not that I was freed entirely by one childhood experience. For example, I was supposed to like my Aunt Bunny, and I felt guilty that I didn't. I felt especially guilty when she died and I wasn't sad about it. Since this particular aunt was never nice to me, why should I have felt guilty for not liking her? Well, my parents had told me that I should—I must—like my relatives. "After all, she's your *aunt*." But after all, she was *mean*.

Your Own Choices In Your Own Way

If you've ever felt uncomfortable about questioning the authority figures in your life, or you've made a wise decision that others thought was dumb or wrong or would surely lead to disaster, then you know that the so-called wrong thing may be exactly right for you. That's what this book is all about. But because the conventional choice so often *is* the right one, you may have trouble recognizing those times when it isn't. You may have a deep desire to do something, but dismiss it as wrong, odd, unrealistic, or something your parents (or husband, wife, boss, or friend) wouldn't approve of. Any number of reactions can squelch your independent thinking.

In the chapters that follow you'll have the opportunity to examine your attitudes in many areas of life. You'll learn how truisms may have ruled your choices—in ways you might not have realized. You'll also learn to listen carefully when others give you advice—solicited or unsolicited—and to question it. Is the advice based on a generally accepted rule, or is the person taking your individual situation into consideration? Does this person give the same advice in just about every situation that comes along?

Does It Take Two?

A woman I know stayed in a marriage for twenty years because she thought she must be half the problem—her father told her over and over this was true. She went to counseling, she read all the advice books, she tried talking about the problem. She tried everything. Her husband never moved an inch. It was in his best interests for her to continue believing that something was wrong with her. Conventional wisdom tells us that it takes two people to make a marriage fail. Maybe that's true most of the time, but I know it isn't true all the time. If my friend was at fault at all, it might have been for putting up with this passive-aggressive man for so long, her father's advice notwithstanding.

In the past twenty to thirty years, we have seen numerous changes in the way we think about life. The major political and social movements—civil rights, women's liberation, environmentalism, and peace and disarmament—have greatly contributed to the push to make independent choices. I've known families that experienced great strain because a son or daughter took to the picket lines. Marriages have broken up over a women's refusal to squelch her own desire to do meaningful work in the world. I've even seen families cut off all contact with a relative who married outside his or her religion or race. Untold suffering is caused when people turn away from others in disapproval over choices. And, it often takes a strong person to simply stand up for what appears to be the right choice at the time.

Who Admires a Conformist Anyway?

We are constantly faced with a paradox. On the one hand, we are fed certain truisms, conventional wisdom, rigid rules for what is right and what is wrong, codes of behavior and taste, and other attitudes we are expected to conform to. On the other hand, the most widely admired people are those who seem to "march to the beat of their own drum." "They broke the mold when they made him," someone will say in an admiring tone, or, "She sure is a one-of-a-kind person."

How often do you hear someone say, "What a guy, he always conforms"? Or when was the last time you heard, "The thing I like about that woman is the way she follows all the rules and does exactly what is expected of her without asking questions"?

When you begin exploring ways to make decisions your own way, with your own best interests at heart, keep these statements in mind. As you slog along trying to satisfy all the critical voices, do you really believe that you'll be admired for it? Remember, the most revered and admired people in history are those who often did the so-called "wrong" thing because they knew it was right.

When the Wrong Thing Really Is Wrong

Some years ago, I worked with individuals who were on probation after serving a prison sentence. Jack had been in prison for several years after being convicted for selling drugs and for armed robbery. Jack was a young man who acted as if he were truly interested in rehabilitation—many of these young clients were. But, after we'd worked together for a while, Jack began to reveal his true attitudes. This young man had been raised in poverty and abuse, leaving him with the attitude that he was owed something for the hardship he'd endured. "I have as much right to be rich as the next guy," he'd say. Unfortunately, Jack actually believed that stealing was okay because it was his way to become rich. He was even willing to take the chance of getting caught again, because stealing was his career, his way of life.

In Jack's case, the wrong thing really was the wrong thing. We can't sit back and romanticize about Jack and say that he was simply following his own star. No matter how hard I tried to convince him that his attitudes were morally and ethically wrong, he remained unconvinced. A few months after his release from prison, he was back in again. I sometimes wonder if he still thinks he's justified in going against the rules.

Sexual decisions are another area where certain obvious rules apply. While there have always been sexually transmitted diseases, the AIDS issue has made our sexual choices even more crucial. No one is ever justified in risking another person's health, and even life, in some selfish pursuit of momentary pleasure. Although many of my clients have made so-called incorrect sexual decisions, those I mention here have generally made them in a context in which others were informed, and not put at undue risk.

I mention these examples in which wrong is wrong because I don't want anyone to misinterpret what I say in these pages and believe I am sanctioning careless, irresponsible choices. Nor am I suggesting that anyone who has deep religious or humanistic beliefs that certain things are *always* wrong, change those convictions in any way. Our convictions about issues are an integral part of who we are, and going against them just to be different doesn't lead us to wise choices.

LOOKING WITHIN

I believe that most answers to life's dilemmas come from within our own minds and hearts. Every time we make a decision, we are learning something about ourselves and our values and beliefs. When we feel good about a choice—even if it is difficult or painful—we have usually acted out of our own deepest wisdom. Even if we make a mistake, we usually gain insight into ourselves.

When a decision doesn't sit well with us, when we end up in a stew or in a constant state of regret, we can often identify a reason that has some connection to the conventional view of right and wrong or wise and foolish. Again, this isn't *always* the case, but it happens often enough that we should evaluate our choice and ask ourselves why we were compelled to make a decision that left us unhappy, fuming, unsatisfied, sad, and so on.

I'm going to take you on a journey through many areas of life—love; marriage; sex; relationships with parents, children, siblings and other relatives; money; careers; appearance issues; and some more general attitudes about the way we live. Some of the stories are on the light side; others are serious and the decisions involved were significant and life changing. You will learn about some of my clients and others I've known who, at some point said, "I'm doing it my own way."

Two

Whose Attitudes Are These Anyway?

Nick "confessed" that he often fantasized about having sex with his very attractive sister-in-law. In his heart and soul, however, he knew he would never attempt to act out his fantasy. Still, much emotional energy was squandered in feeling guilty about even having such thoughts. Clearly, his sister-in-law was "forbidden fruit," and he put great effort into trying to end these thoughts.

Betty, a first-time mother, felt terribly guilty because she sometimes felt resentful and angry about the disruption the new baby had brought to her life. She also resented her husband because he seemed to enjoy the baby so much; sometimes she even felt jealous of the time and attention he showered on their daughter. She was so angry with herself for having these feelings that she was missing out on all the pleasure she got from the new baby most of the time.

Carl loved his brother, Jim, but was not happy for him when he bought an expensive new car and built his own home. He found himself avoiding Jim, which added guilt to his other array of feelings.

Mitzi was outraged when she thought about the fact that her friend, Joy, who is neither as pretty nor as talented as she is, became a well-known actress. They see each other often, and Mitzi tries her best to cover up her anger.

Joe was furious when Bryan was promoted and he was not. He went through all the gracious motions, leading Bryan to believe Joe was genuinely pleased for him. But underneath it all Joe still seethed—even though he knew in his deepest being that Bryan did a better job and was a harder worker.

Situations like these arise in our lives so often, we could view them as everyday events. As a therapist, I see that the feelings involved typically result from deeply held attitudes and beliefs. However, more often than not, people are unable to say where the belief came from or why they continue to let it heap guilt on them. Some of these attitudes and beliefs influence our decision-making process. If these attitudes remain unquestioned and guide our lives, they can lead us in directions we may not want to go.

As you read about the people in this chapter, examine your own attitudes about the situations, thoughts, and feelings presented. Do you know where you acquired these attitudes that guide not only your actions, but result in negative judgments about yourself for even having certain thoughts and feelings?

IF I THINK IT, IT MUST BE SO

Almost everyone has a tendency to blame themselves for so-called "bad" thoughts. In fact, all the people listed above had spent so much time berating themselves for unpleasant thoughts and feelings that they had little mental energy left to consider what the thoughts and feelings were telling them. Nor were they able to examine where the self-berating tendency came from.

In Nick's case, a real or imagined authority figure was looking over his shoulder, telling him in no uncertain terms that he was "bad, bad, bad" for having sexual fantasies about his sister-in-law.

Because the condemning voice was so loud, Nick was not able to separate his thoughts from his actions.

Nick was relieved when, after a few sessions of therapy with me, I suggested that he stop repressing his thoughts and feelings—because thoughts and feelings are neither bad nor good, they're simply messengers that tell us about ourselves. In a matter of days, Nick found he was thinking less and less about his sister-in-law. When the fantasies did start they were far less intense, mainly because he had stopped fighting with himself every step of the way. He was then able to go on with the issues that he originally came to therapy to address. Resolving these personal issues then led to a better relationship with his wife.

Stop to consider how you acquired the notion that certain thoughts are bad—perhaps even as bad as actions. Did your parents tell you that it wasn't nice to be jealous? So when you were nine years old you tried to stop thinking about how much you envied your best friend's nicer birthday party or more expensive presents? Maybe you thought you were bad if you disliked this friend, even for a day or two.

A Bundle of Feelings

Were you told that if you chose something, you had to love it—all the time, without qualification? Betsy, a new mother, was adjusting to an entirely different way of life. Before her baby was born, she had been a doctor in a community hospital. Now she was spending all her time taking care of the new baby. She had expected to love every minute of it, and her mother had told her how wonderful her days of caring for her daughter would be. Her mother also told her that her new life would be so wonderful that she'd never even think about her career.

In her old life, Betsy was a respected professional, someone who people came to for help. Her colleagues respected her as a superb diagnostician. Now, a few months into motherhood, she discovered that she missed her patients and the company of adults. Her husband, also a doctor, seemed to have the best of both worlds. He was able to continue working in his profession and enjoy the baby too. For several months, Betsy saw herself as a martyr. Because she had given up her career, she thought the world and her husband viewed her differently. Worse yet, she felt guilty for becoming resentful toward every person—especially her mother— who told her how lucky she was.

It came as quite a shock to Betsy when her husband confided that he was jealous of her. He wished that he could have a break from the professional grind and stay home with the baby. He also envied her ability to nurse the baby. So he ended up feeling very childish and guilty because she seemed to have the better deal. He, in turn, was very surprised when Betsy told him that she envied him his freedom to continue working and just have fun with their daughter.

Betsy had a difficult time understanding that many new parents experience some resentment about the responsibility they have taken on. No matter how loved and wanted a baby is, new parents naturally will feel overwhelmed and may occasionally long for the life they left behind. It took quite a while for Betsy to accept her own passing thoughts without also experiencing great guilt over them. When she and her husband could talk openly about their mutual feelings of envy and resentment, they were able to clear the air between them.

In this case, honesty led to a new solution. Once the baby was weaned, Betsy went back to work part time and her husband cut back his practice by almost a third. He then had time to take care of the baby while Betsy worked at the hospital. It was an ideal solution for this couple. But, hard as it is to believe, this decision caused great commotion in their families. These "experts" thought that the husband was becoming a wimp. Just imagine— a *doctor* cutting back *his* practice. If Betsy and her husband had listened to their families, they'd be right back where they started.

Quit the Self-Berating and Surprises Appear

When we stop fighting jealousy and resentment and quit telling ourselves how bad we are, we can gain insight and bring new wisdom into important areas of our lives. For example, when Carl stopped trying to pretend that he didn't feel jealous about his brother's possessions, he was able to uncover the real source of resentment, his father's favoritism toward the first-born son. Carl's sisters had resented their father's attitude toward the oldest son, but were able to accept it as a fact, break away from their father, and build lives based more on their own values. Carl's resentment had more to do with his failure to please this unpleasable man than with any dissatisfaction with his own house or car.

When Bryan began examining his resentment of Joe, he realized that he might always envy Joe's professional talents. Granted, this may not coincide with the conventional notion of what is nice and what isn't, but the fact is, we don't have nice thoughts all the time. Because of his job situation, Bryan had little choice but to be outwardly pleasant to Joe. The working environment required this ability to pretend, and that's what Joe concluded he had to do. There are some situations in which pretending to like something or someone is the best course of action.

On the other hand, in certain situations, particularly one involving a close friend, pretending can be harmful. Mitzi spent months pretending to be happy for her more successful best friend. The more she pretended, the more she began to fantasize revenge. Resentment and revenge often go hand in hand. Rather than feeling guilty over her fantasies, Mitzi needed to accept that a part of her couldn't feel love toward her friend. Who ever said that we have to be happy for others all the time? When we can't, we can't.

We usually want revenge when we've actually been harmed by

another person. If we let ourselves fantasize about getting revenge, we usually find that it wears itself out. And remember, thoughts are not the same as actions. In many cases, taking revenge could do real harm and, of course, I don't recommend it. However, you are not a bad person because you have wished harm to another person who has hurt you—you are simply being human. Most people are able to eventually let go of their need for revenge.

Look to Yourself—Later

In addition to being taught to believe that thoughts are bad, many of us also were taught that anger is a bad emotion, one to be avoided at all times. In order to avoid being outraged at other people, we are taught to look to ourselves to determine how we caused the situation we're now angry about.

We may need to do this in many cases, but not necessarily in every situation that occurs. Let's say you accidentally leave your handbag in your car. Someone breaks into your car and steals it. You're furious, you feel violated, and you think about what you'd do to the thief if you could get your hands on him or her. Some people will be in this furious state and then go on and take care of the practical consequences. But there are others who will say, "It's all my fault because I left my handbag in the car." They are filled with self-blame and may have difficulty carrying out necessary tasks such as filing a police report and calling credit card companies. The fact that the thief was wrong—under any circumstances—is lost on them while they indulge in self-blame.

Sidnie blamed herself for her mother's death—if only she had taken better care of her mother while she recovered from her cancer surgery. Arthur blamed himself because his son took candy from the convenience store down the street. Mary blamed herself because her husband ran off with a woman who liked to cook and provided him with better meals. In all three cases, the individuals were furious—with a mother for dying and abandoning a daughter, with a son for being a sneak, and with a husband for being a shallow jerk. They felt so guilty about their anger that they turned all the blame on themselves.

But it seems to me that if they allowed themselves some space to be angry and even think vengeful thoughts, they then would be able to sort through the self-blame issues with greater ease and clarity. Sidnie was angry with her mother for dying, but it was more acceptable to blame herself. Where did that attitude come from? Whose attitude is it? (Some people claim that a degree of guilt is always present when a loved one dies. So if you don't feel it, there's something wrong with you. Have you absorbed this particular belief? What are the implications of it in your life?)

Arthur had great support from the "experts" when he blamed himself for his son's stealing. Authorities love it when parents accept responsibility for everything. If he dared to say, "What a bratty thing for my son to do—I'm going to set him straight right away," he'd be accused of denying his own responsibility for his son's behavior. I don't agree. Arthur's anger at his son seems like a natural reaction.

Mary has always firmly believed that she's responsible for everything, from homelessness on our streets to her husband's philandering. She spent months crying over this man's desertion, all the while believing that she should have been a better cook. One day, after months of this self-blame, she had a random and sudden thought about smashing a meat loaf in his face. She imagined how he'd look with the food stuck to his nose. This thought amused her so much that she started laughing to herself. (Mary was on the bus at the time, so she forced herself to suppress her urge to giggle, for fear of being thought crazy. Who ever said we can't laugh out loud at a private joke or thought?)

Over the next few days, Mary's revenge fantasies involved food—from pouring pasta sauce on her husband's clothes to his death from food poisoning. Mary enjoyed herself and felt little guilt over these fantasies because she had no intention of acting on them. They never even became part of her thought process. Mary has a good sense of humor and she found these images quite funny—in a vengeful sort of way.

A year after he left, Mary's husband showed up at her door one evening and said he wanted her back. "I just made a mistake," he said. Mary listened with a degree of guarded sympathy to his tale of renewed devotion to her. Then, true to form, Arthur asked her to fix him some dinner. She started laughing as she demanded that he get out. She eventually learned that his new woman had thrown him out and his empty stomach led him back to Mary. All his stories of devotion were "cooked up" to gain her sympathy. If Mary hadn't gone through her revenge fantasies she might have stayed stuck in self-blame. And, she might have let this needy, "hungry" husband back into her life.

If you're the kind of person who blames yourself for everything, examine where you acquired that attitude. Chances are, you absorbed the idea that anger, envy, resentment, and the desire for revenge are "bad," and the only other alternative is to blame yourself. While in therapy, Mary did look to herself and accept responsibility, not so much for the breakup of her marriage, but for choosing that man in the first place.

There is an enormous difference between taking responsibility and self-blame. Blaming ourselves usually involves either extreme martyrdom or self-hate. Responsibility means that we acknowledge a situation and decide how we could have made a different choice. For example, Arthur had to take responsibility for the fact that his son was stealing, but that's entirely different from blaming himself, as if it were his own hand reaching out to the candy shelf.

IT'S NOT ALL BLACK AND WHITE

One the most difficult adjustments we must make in life is understanding that we may not feel great about all our choices. We often may be faced with the least unpleasant or least compromising choice. When Gloria came to me she was suffering from two seemingly conflicting reactions. Her daughter had recently died after a long bout with cancer. This loss was so painful that on many days she could barely get out of bed. Gloria had dropped everything to take care of her child and now she didn't have a job—or much of a life at all. She found herself resenting her daughter for leaving her and she felt guilty about that feeling. She also experienced guilt over the resentment she'd felt during the long months of caring for her daughter. It had taken a great physical and emotional toll to devote all her time to this dying young woman.

The fact is, Gloria may always suffer from her painful loss, and she may always have some regret over giving up her own life. But, when she looked carefully at the decisions she had made, she wouldn't have changed anything. Sometimes we simply must adjust to the fact we will be ambivalent.

For instance, nowadays a woman who returns to work after the birth of a child will almost always be ambivalent about the situation. This is generally true whether a woman must work or whether she chooses to. But let's remember that only a generation ago, women were expected to give up their careers for husbands and children, and the need to work often represented failure on the part of the "provider."

Too often, child development specialists, psychologists, doctors, and others who deal with mental health issues, tell women that they must "feel good" about their decision. However, this may be too much to ask. In real life, most women feel fine about this decision (whichever one it is) on some days, and on other days, they feel rotten. They may never be completely comfortable with either choice, and this is the most realistic adjustment. Furthermore, some women may always resent that their husbands don't feel the least bit guilty for going off to work. Other women may resent their husbands because they didn't have to give up satisfying work to raise the kids.

Watching For Extremes

I believe most people find that resentment lessens, fantasies wear out, and thoughts of revenge eventually quiet down if they stop trying to force their thinking into models they have absorbed along the way. These people make a clear distinction between thoughts and actions. They may even enjoy their revenge fantasies, as Mary did, knowing that they aren't harming anyone.

If, however, you find yourself obsessed with certain kinds of thoughts, or if you aren't sure you can draw the line at thoughts and feel moved to action, then you may need professional help. A safe, nonjudgmental place to talk about these troublesome thoughts may provide some relief. I urge you to seek help if your thoughts are making your day-to-day life difficult or unpleasant much of the time.

The Power of Anger and Revenge

The people who tell us that it's not nice to be angry or to want revenge may overlook or underestimate the motivation these mental states often provide. Haven't you ever wanted to accomplish something so you could say, "I showed him," or, "She thought she was better, well look at me now."

If we're honest with ourselves we usually feel exquisite satisfaction by doing something that others said was impossible. I once had a friend whose family discouraged her interest in art—in fact they often ridiculed it at family gatherings. When she was offered her first one-person show, she sent invitations for the opening night reception to all her family members. As she addressed each one, she felt, as the saying goes, "unholy glee." She showed them, all right. She had even more fun when her father and brothers watched as a collector purchased one of her paintings for three thousand dollars.

When Ken was passed over for a promotion, he was furious and determined that he would become a better salesman than his boss. Many experts would say that anger isn't a good motivator, but in Ken's case, it worked. Within two years, he did have a better sales record, and over the course of the following years, Ken's focus changed—and he found himself motivated less by anger than by the challenge and the exhiliration he felt when he broke into a new territory.

Many a divorced person has picked him or herself up, motivated to create a rich fulfilling life, in order to prove a former partner wrong. In these cases, living well is indeed the best revenge. By the time the person is comfortable and living a better life, the revenge motive is usually long forgotten. So it hardly matters if revenge was the original motivator—and it probably wasn't the *only* motivator anyway.

I'd be very skeptical of anyone who tells you that you should be motivated only by love or by selfless desire. This might be a worthy goal, but to deny that so-called negative things sometimes move us into action is unrealistic.

Taking a Second Look

I can't even count the number of clients I've had who believed they couldn't quit working on a project once they started it, couldn't fail at an undertaking, and most certainly couldn't just walk away from troubles—literally leave them behind. Since it took me years to figure out that I didn't have to finish reading a book I didn't enjoy, and I'm permitted to leave the theater in the middle of a movie, I understand these people. They apparently received many of the same messages I did.

If you feel imprisoned by your decisions, then take a second look at where and how you acquired the attitudes with which you made them. You might be very surprised by the way you have hung on to certain ideas, simply because you haven't thought out the other options. How would you behave in the scenarios presented below? What are your initial reactions to the decisions these people made? Examine your thoughts as they come up to see if you would have similar struggles.

Never Quit, No Matter What

Sam had a master's degree in history and a good job as a researcher for a large corporation. The goal of getting his doctorate still loomed large, however, and despite his active family life, he enrolled in a tough Ph.D. program. After two semesters he had exhausted himself and he resented his job, his children, and even his wife. Furthermore, he didn't like the program and since he'd never wanted an academic career, the advanced degree would bring him little more than prestige. He thought about quitting, but he just couldn't bring himself to do it. "Finish what you start, finish what you start," went through his head like a mantra. When that wore itself out, "you'll be sorry, you'll be sorry," went through his head.

In the middle of his third semester, Sam was flat on his back for three weeks with a serious case of pneumonia. As a result, he failed a class and was told he'd have to take it over again. The very thought of taking that dreaded class again was distressing and depressing. He'd almost rather stay ill, he thought. While in this unhappy state he dropped out of the program, and sure enough, over the next few weeks he was sorry. At least part of him was. Underlying all the expected regret was a tremendous sense of relief, which he finally admitted to his closest friends and to his wife. He later told me that he was shocked by how supportive these people were. "They wondered how long I'd go on with the grind that I had clearly begun to loath more and more."

At fifty, Sam used this experience to quit some other things too. He started a small consulting business, which eventually became a full-time endeavor, and the next year, he quit going to a church whose teachings emphasized guilt and sin. (That pleased his wife, who hadn't ever liked the church, but it horrified his rigid parents. But then, they had always told him that finishing what one starts is a must, no matter what the personal cost.)

How Long Is Enough?

Sharon is a warm, sensitive woman in her twenties, who had always wanted to be a nurse. Throughout her training she imagined what it would be like to finally work in a hospital, where, she assumed, she would truly be helping people. Disillusionment came early. In her first job, she found herself very disappointed in the emotionally cold environment. Furthermore, she believed that many of the patients were receiving dangerous treatments, and her ideas to help reduce patients' discomfort were ignored—even ridiculed. She left that position for another that unfortunately presented the same kind of problems.

Sharon's family and friends counseled her to stick with nursing; after all, they said, she shouldn't "waste" her training. They also can't seem to accept that kind of "mistake." Her brother has told her to be a fighter not a quitter.

At this point, Sharon has not been able to make a decision. She continues to work at a job she doesn't care about, all the while trying to decide what to do. I'm hoping that with support, she will be able to leave nursing, even if only temporarily. Perhaps she needs some experience in another field, which could help moderate her high ideals, and help her accept the realities of any profession. She could always return to nursing later on. As her therapist, I don't see the point in her family's insistence that she stick with a job that is making her so unhappy. However, this is her decision, and she'll have to make it in her own way.

For Worse or Worse?

Judy and Peter had been unhappily married for twenty-seven years, during which years of counseling with four different therapists hadn't brought good results. Everyone, including their latest therapist, thought they should work it out and stay together. Meanwhile, both were having affairs and rarely saw each other except at their weekly therapy session and family gatherings. From all the "experts" in their lives (including so-called best friends) they heard such things as:

- You have a shared history, you can't give it up.
- Your adult children will be shattered.
- It's a cruel world out there.
- Any companionship is better than none.
- You'll both be poor.
- What about your grandchildren?

Peter finally said he didn't care about any of this and walked out. Judy and Peter saw a mediator and worked out an amicable property settlement. Their children, while sad, also said they understood that their parents had been mismatched from the beginning. Both found much more happiness and contentment after their divorce. Peter has not remarried yet, and doubts that he ever will; Judy moved in with the man she was having an affair with and with whom she is much more compatible. Judy and Peter have only one regret: that they didn't part much sooner.

FAILURE OR LEARNING?

The same people who believe that sham marriages should remain intact usually preach the philosophy that failure is a catastrophe to be avoided. "If at first you don't succeed, try, try again," is one their favorite clichés. They also like to talk about excellence—"If a thing is worth doing, it's worth doing well." Well, maybe, but maybe not.

Certainly it's good to try things that you've always wanted to do. One of my friends always wanted to paint—until she tried it. Not only was she awkward and slow, she found her mind drifting to other things when the instructor demonstrated various techniques. My friend desperately wanted to quit the class, but she believed that she couldn't leave it behind until she had succeeded. In other words, once she'd proved that she *could* paint, she wouldn't have to.

Into this twisted situation came her young grandson who proudly announced one day that he was a lousy soccer player and was quitting the team before he hurt himself or, as he put it, "got asked to leave." She started to tell him that he shouldn't quit until he was good enough to show others that he was leaving on his own terms. "The sentence was almost out of my mouth when I realized how insane it was," she said. "So I paused and told him that I was stopping this silly painting, too. He reassured me that I'd find something I was good at—he certainly intended to try another sport."

Her grandson is the kind of "expert" I like. He'd given soccer a try, which is good, and he determined that he'd try something else. Failure often can teach us about our true capabilities. My friend who wanted to paint enjoyed art and went back to collecting the work of up-and-coming artists. Her grandson eventually found that long-distance running was his sports niche. I know other children for whom all sports are a trial and if they choose to avoid the whole thing, I'd encourage them to find other activities more to their liking.

Too often, children attempt certain sports or other activities just to please mom and dad. They may stick with a sport long after they've begun to hate it, because they have the "don't quit" message deeply ingrained. This attitude then carries over to adult life. Perhaps you can identify with this belief, and if you can, probe within and find out where you learned it.

If we give something our best shot, what more can we ask of ourselves? Jill had always wanted to be an actress. As many people in this situation do, she worked as a waitress as she made the rounds to auditions and agents. After nearly three years, she had been offered only one small part that she didn't perform well. She gave it her best, but it didn't work out. In this case, failure brought a dream to an end—but she knew she'd never look back and regret that she hadn't tried.

I always encourage clients to consider all their options before they quit a profession or job, leave a marriage, give up a dream, and so on. Most of us occasionally choose projects, partners, or careers for which we are unsuited. And if we "fail" and admit it, then that's the best thing that can happen.

Quit, Fail, and Leave

Henry was a lonely gay man who couldn't seem to find even a shred of happiness after his long-term life partner died. He had few people with whom he could discuss his situation, because most of his acquaintances were coworkers who didn't know he was gay. At first, he tried getting involved in the gay community by joining a few organizations in his town. Still, he was isolated and lonely. He began thinking about making a big change.

When Henry came to me he had an urge to sell his house and move across the country in order to make a completely fresh start. But his sister kept saying, "You can't leave your troubles behind, they'll only follow you. Geographic cures never work." But after we talked for a few weeks, Henry decided his idea was worth trying. A few months later he wrote to me and said that he was happily settled in Seattle, had made new friends, and was working part time until he found a job in his field. He wasn't lonely anymore and was no longer haunted by the memories of his friend's painful death.

Making a Break For It

Mark and Anna were raised in different religious faiths. Mark's parents insisted that they marry within his religion, but they chose to have the wedding according to Anna's tradition. Although they reluctantly came to the wedding, Mark's father complained every minute and his mother cried so much that one of the guests suggested they call a doctor. During the first couple of years of the newlyweds' marriage, Mark's parents, who didn't even like Anna, intruded in their lives and manipulated situations so they could be with the couple often. Mark and Anna began to argue over what to do about his parents.

In desperation, Mark arranged a transfer to another city, and they happily moved, eager to leave their troubles behind. They were told by family members, Anna's family included, that this solution would never work. However, it did work out very well. The couple found they could get along with Mark's parents for limited visits, as long as the in-laws stayed in a hotel rather than in their home. As often happens, Mark's parents softened toward Anna and as the years passed, family relationships improved. I believe the distance helped.

It seems very natural to me that people want to get away from places they associate with painful incidents, or where they can't fully be themselves. Sometimes people leave troubles behind because of a failed romance, and I've seen many clients move away to pursue a new relationship. In many cases, this has brought beneficial changes in other areas of their lives as well. A change of location won't change everything, but I've seen situations in which it truly meant a fresh start. Our country would never have been settled if millions of people hadn't left their troubles behind and made new starts. Tell that to the experts.

RESOLUTION MAY NOT BE POSSIBLE

Most of us desire to resolve the important issues in our lives. We generally believe the concept that "the truth will set us free," which has merit much of the time. But there has been a tendency in recent years for mental health professionals to insist that every problem must be resolved—or it will come back to haunt the client at a later time. I don't think this is a wise trend. The idea presupposes that every issue can be resolved, a pipe dream in itself. Furthermore, there are times when we simply must turn our attention to other things and live with the lack of resolution. In certain cases, trying to confront or resolve issues, or even search for the truth, can result in new, even more disturbing problems.

Agnes came to me after working with a therapist who insisted that she confront her father, who had sexually abused her. At age eighty-six, he was frail and not mentally alert most of the time. The idea of confronting him was unacceptable to Agnes, especially since she had been feeling so much better. For her, resolution had come with talking about the abuse and learning to feel good about herself in spite of it. Sure, she felt anger and even hatred toward her father, but she wanted to leave it at that. The therapist who encouraged the confrontation was basing her advice on what *she* thought was best in such situations. But this solution was not necessarily good for Agnes, and I'm glad she had the courage to search her own heart and decide what was best for her.

When we think about resolving issues and searching for the truth at all costs, we may be mislead by talk-show stories of confrontations that worked out well. For example, on talk shows we may see reunions with adoptees and birth parents that later result in huge family gatherings and the creation of strong bonds. Nowadays, adopted children often are encouraged to search for their birth mothers because, they are told, there will always be an empty spot within them if they don't learn the truth. I've even heard professionals say that the lives of adopted children are incomplete if they don't "resolve" the issue of early abandonment. Well, maybe so, but maybe not. This depends entirely on the individual.

A Disappointing Reunion

Not long ago, I talked with a young woman who, on the advice of her college advisor, undertook a search for her birth mother. She did this not out of any particular desire to meet the woman, but because her advisor had told her that future problems could be avoided if she resolved this issue while she was still young. The search took a year, and this young woman was far more disturbed by the experience of finding her birth mother than she was by not knowing anything about her. The woman was mean, not happy to see her, and in short, told her to "get lost." Three years later, she now regrets ever taking that advice. "I wish I'd left well enough alone and had not allowed myself to be convinced that something was a problem when it wasn't. I'd always been quite happy with my family and didn't feel incomplete in any way. But my advisor didn't believe me."

This is only one case, and I realize that many people find that such reunions help satisfy natural curiosity and resolve some issues. Some people meet other relatives and become part of a second family. This is wonderful when it happens, but it can turn out badly too, something that these searchers may not be warned about.

My advice is always to think very carefully before trying to resolve something that someone else told you is an important issue. You're the best judge of what needs resolution and closure in your life—and what doesn't.

SOME ATTITUDES AREN'T YOUR OWN

Because we are influenced by experts and our family and friends, we may find ourselves in confusing situations where we're receiving advice from all sides. Many people really believe that there is only one right answer for just about every dilemma. This belief can make it difficult for you to make a choice you instinctively know is right for you, because when your decision goes against conventional wisdom and majority opinion, when your choice isn't compatible with this *one* right option, you may be at odds with those close to you. However, you can learn to make decisions your own way and be happier for it.

In the next chapter, we'll explore some principles that will help you break out of old patterns and make decisions independent of the opinions and beliefs others hold dear.

THREE

Learning To Make Choices Your Own Way

"For heaven's sake, don't marry *that* guy!"
"Don't take that job—it won't lead anywhere."
"Buying that house would be the worst
  mistake you could make."
"You do that, and you'll sure live to regret it."

It often seems that everyone has something to say about the choices we make. Sometimes we go against our own instincts because we believe that if so many people think we're making a mistake, then perhaps we're wrong and they're right. In chapter 2, we talked about the common attitudes most of us acquire as we move through life, attitudes that can adversely affect decisions large and small. Now let's move on and discuss the ways in which we can make choices that aren't based solely on truisms, conventional wisdom, or the popular opinion of the day.

TRUSTING OUR INNER TRUTH

It isn't always easy to trust—or even identify—our own deepest truth, the wisdom about what is right for us, wisdom that is rooted deep within us. Much of our internal sense of what is right or correct is a product of our cultural and familial upbringing, which is then modified by our own life experience and the personality and disposition we were born with.

Many individuals deny any feelings that are contrary to what they have been taught is good or right; they literally silence their own inner voices and conform to outside voices, even when it is uncomfortable to do so.

Some choices we would like to make may go against ideas so deeply ingrained that choosing a different path may be next to impossible. For example, if you were taught that you must obey all rules without question, you might carry this message into situations where obeying a rule leads you down a path filled with blind submission to mistaken authority. We see illustrations of this everywhere, but people who follow authority with a sense of complete abandon may not even be aware they have an inner truth.

Sorting through attitudes, beliefs, opinions, and feelings sometimes involves seeking out authorities—but there are times when it means avoiding them. There are situations where we must avoid negative people, those who believe almost everything we do is fraught with danger. I've observed that negative people may not be worried about danger at all. Instead, they may be ignorant about the situation or may even be jealous that someone else isn't afraid to be an independent thinker.

I have seen many people gather strength, courage, and resolve only to have it torn down because others belittle their ideas or speak disparagingly of them. Sometimes it's better to keep our own counsel until we are ready to act, even if it means enduring negative responses from others after the fact. Ultimately, we have to conquer our fears and do what feels right for us, or we will always be living through the attitudes and ideas of others.

SO, WHAT WOULD YOU DO?

If we want to be free from the admonitions of well-meaning people, we have to develop confidence in our choices. Let's start by examining some situations in which the person involved had a number of options. The scenarios below illustrate the ways that particular individuals sorted through attitudes and beliefs and made their own decisions, free from outside pressure. Put yourself in each person's shoes for a minute and see what choice you would have made.

Nan Finds Her Way

Nan was a generous, caring, and creative woman who loved art and music. As a child, she had wanted to spend all her free time painting and drawing, but there was no money for art supplies. In addition, her parents thought this was not a particularly useful way to spend her time. Although she took art classes in high school, her family was more interested in her progress in home economics and secretarial courses.

Eventually, after working in an office for several years, Nan met a man who wanted to marry her. There was much rejoicing in Nan's house, because marriage was viewed as her real job. Nan's husband was a combination of traditional and modern. He was traditional in the sense that he believed he was head of the household and held most of the decision-making power. He was modern in that he believed that after the children were in school, Nan should look for another well-paying secretarial job. After she found a job, he thought, she would stop all this art nonsense that took up so much time.

Nan was unhappy with the dilemma she found herself in. Her husband was an excellent father to their two sons. They had a life filled with activity and warm relationships with family and friends. She loved her husband despite his nasty attitude toward her interest in art. Still, the once peaceful household was threatening to erupt.

Nan talked to her minister, who told her, "Your family should come first. It's your job to create a peaceful home. If you are distracted by your art, then you should cut back on the time you spend on it."

When Nan talked to her mother, she said, "Don't be so obvious about it. Don't talk about it. Just go along with him on this. Do your art when he's not around so he won't be irritated or threatened by it. We all have to manipulate a little to make a marriage work."

Nan's close friend, June, also an artist, said, "He has a lot of nerve calling your art a bunch of nonsense. I'd leave him in a minute. No one would belittle me like that."

Another of Nan's friends said, "He seems so insecure. Maybe he's jealous of your art because you're so good at it and other people give you attention. Maybe he's just a baby who needs to grow up. But I wouldn't give up on him just yet."

So, what would you do if you were in Nan's shoes? What are her options? What attitudes are revealed in the advice and reactions that others gave her? Some of the opinions seem fairly superficial, but others reveal attitudes that run deep within our culture.

Nan's minister and her mother both revealed their belief that it is a woman's job to make a marriage work and whatever it takes to do that is the "right" thing—even if it means denying one's own talents and interests or hiding them. Here we have an example of a person who believes in the supremacy of the patriarchy and expresses the "head of the household" mentality. Nan's mother agrees with that attitude, but also advises Nan to manipulate her husband if necessary. Additionally, we have the two friends, one who expresses a "throw the bum out" attitude; the other is more analytical and believes that perhaps Nan can change her husband's attitude.

After many bouts of depression and anxiety, Nan entered counseling. She learned that from an early age, she had abandoned many of her desires and talents, not just her art work. She had been afraid to speak up for what she wanted because children's opinions, especially those expressed by girls, were devalued. In order to get along, Nan became the classic "good little girl," who later tried to be a "good little wife."

All along, Nan attempted to repress her true feelings and accept that she shouldn't have so-called selfish interests. Consequently, she felt guilty every time she was drawn back to her watercolors and charcoal. No matter what she did, she was unhappy and unfulfilled. And Nan's husband could issue orders, but that didn't make him feel very good either. Like many men who feel threatened, he knew how talented Nan was and he also was aware that she was a very strong person—perhaps even stronger than him in some ways.

Nan worked extremely hard in therapy and it took more than two years for her to recognize that her desires and needs counted and were valid. At first, Nan's family didn't like the fact that she refused some of their requests. Her mother called her selfish. Her husband called her stubborn. Even her children wondered why their mother was refusing to wait on them. Over and over, she did things that she was raised to believe were "wrong": questioning authority, stating her needs, refusing to be a doormat for others to walk on. At the same time, others seemed to have no understanding of Nan's struggle. Her artist friend, for example, still thought she should leave her marriage—what other choice was there?

As the years went on, Nan's husband adjusted to the idea that she would have her own life and interests outside of the marriage. When she finally understood that her own negative attitudes toward herself had been in the way, she was able to communicate her deep need to express herself. Perhaps her second friend was right. Nan's husband was indeed immature and insecure. But Nan loved him and didn't choose to leave. Today, she lives happily with him and her mother still tells Nan she's doing the wrong thing. (Nan's mother never did appreciate creativity and probably never will.)

Arthur and Tami Win Out

Arthur's mother was not even willing to consider that he would marry Tami, a woman who practiced a different religion. In fact, she repeatedly said, "If you marry her I'll lie down in my grave and never get up again." (She had a flair for the dramatic in other areas too.)

For some people, such a decision would be easy. They'd simply ignore disapproving parents and marry the person of their choice. Arthur didn't have such an easy time, mainly because he took his religion very seriously. In fact, he and Tami came to couple's counseling before they were married so they could sort through these family problems. Tami's parents weren't thrilled with their marriage plans either, although neither had threatened to crawl into their graves over it. Those who disapprove of interfaith marriages often do so because they have seen so many fail—the fact that many same-faith marriages also fail seems lost on them.

If you were Arthur or Tami what would you have done? Would you have gone ahead with the marriage, even if it meant your family would not attend? Or, would you have postponed the marriage or perhaps even broken off the engagement?

As their therapist, I was drawn to both Arthur and Tami and thought they were wonderful together. In order to get away from all the negative voices that surrounded them, they took my suggestion and joined a group of people who were facing similar problems. They also talked with a few rabbis and priests who did not take such a hard line on interfaith marriage. (They had already talked with plenty of religious people who were absolutely against it.)

During this process, Arthur learned that other people also had parents who claimed that some action or behavior on their children's part would surely kill them. This threat had been a stumbling block for him; deep down, he wasn't sure that if his mother did die for some reason, it wouldn't be his fault. This was an issue he had to work on before they could continue with their wedding plans. Arthur had to be clear that his mother was responsible for herself.

After working together for a few months, Tami suggested that they set a wedding date, and during their engagement they would continue to talk to their families and hope for their blessing. If it wasn't forthcoming, they would still go ahead with the marriage, but would not be forced to sneak off to marry. Their wedding would be public and all their family and friends would be invited. However, she said, to continue putting off the engagement announcement was unacceptable—the time to make a decision had arrived.

I saw Arthur privately and helped him deal with his mother's threats. A few months later, he informed his mother that he and Tami were being married in four months. She started her usual verbal routine about this situation leading her to an early grave, but Arthur left her home before she finished the sentence. As it stands now, Arthur and Tami have been married for two years. While they are happy together and Tami's parents are part of their lives, Arthur's mother still refuses to come to their home. The couple has learned to live with this unfortunate situation; it is sad and frustrating for both of them, but Arthur knows that he made the correct choice for him.

INVASION OF PRIVACY OR PROTECTION?

Kate was very concerned about her fourteen-year-old daughter, Brittany, who was not only staying out later than she was allowed, but was evasive about where she'd been and who she'd been with. Brittany's grades had fallen drastically, and she often appeared dazed and bleary-eyed.

Kate had allowed Brittany to lock her bedroom door because she had a great respect for privacy. As a child, Kate had not even been allowed to close her bedroom door, and she didn't want to make the same mistake with her own child. However, Kate did have an extra key and knew she could get into the room if she believed she had to. And, she knew Brittany had a diary and that if she read it, she might learn more about her daughter's recent antics.

What would you do? Would you read the diary? Would you find some other way to learn about your child's behavior?

There's a lot to be said for respecting privacy and there is always a loss of trust when we cross those invisible lines. Kate, however, became so concerned about her daughter that she decided to enter the room and read the diary. She felt awful, but justified nonetheless.

In this case, I agree with Kate. She did the so-called "wrong" thing because she needed to protect her child. She learned enough to confront Brittany and to begin to turn the situation around. Other people might have found another way to get the information they needed; still others wouldn't have hesitated to read the diary, believing that young people don't have a right to privacy in the first place. Such decisions have inherent problems, leading me to reiterate that one must follow one's gut.

Taking the Long View

In certain cases, people find that they must go against what seem to be true feelings. For instance, Susan believes that sex outside of marriage is sinful, but her son and his girlfriend, both of whom are in graduate school, live together in an apartment near the university they attend.

If you were Susan, what would you do? Would you accept the situation even if you didn't like it? Would you refuse to see your child? Would you refuse to see the live-in partner? Would you put your child completely out of your life?

"I hate to see them doing this," Susan told me, "because I

know it's a sin. But they don't agree. So, I have two choices—refuse to see him, or see him despite what he's doing."

Susan decided that to refuse to see her son would mean cutting off the relationship, and she wasn't prepared to do that. However, she was under pressure from some of her friends to cut all ties with him unless he "straightened up." One friend said, "If you visit him or have that woman in your home, you'll be condoning what they're doing. You have no choice."

How many times have we been told that we simply have "no choice"—except to do what a well-intentioned "expert" advises? But Susan realized that she did have choices. In her case, she and her son decided that they would agree to disagree. Eventually her son and his partner married and Susan now has a grandchild. Agreeing to disagree worked in this case. She avoided an unpleasant confrontation and a wounding alienation that would have needed healing one day.

That's Not Being a Real Man/Woman

Unlike his wife Karla, a vice president at a major corporation, Stephen hated his job as a salesman. Karla looked forward to going to work and she made a very good salary; Stephen dreaded the sound of the alarm clock. Some months, he barely made his quota and his paycheck was pitiful. One day, their live-in nanny announced she was going back to school and would be leaving them in a few months. Before looking for a replacement, Stephen and Karla thought about the advantages of Stephen leaving his job and staying home with their two toddlers.

When they mentioned this idea to their pediatrician, he advised against it. "Your boy will have a distorted image of manhood, a bad role model," he said in a somber voice. Stephen's father had a different point of view: "Seems to me it's a good solution. No more strangers raising the kids and Karla makes good money." On the other hand, Karla's father wondered what kind of man would let a woman support him. And, Karla's friend Betts, a daycare teacher, warned that the children would love

Stephen more than they loved Karla. For her part, Karla thought it was a great option and she especially liked the idea that one of them would be at home full time.

So, who's right? Depends on your point of view, doesn't it? All the authority figures, professional or not, had a solution for a problem that wasn't theirs to begin with. No matter what Karla and Stephen decided, they were certain to displease someone.

So Stephen gave notice at his office (and found much disapproval there as well) and took on the job of caring for the family. After a year, he realized what was involved in homemaking and child care, and set about finding another job and a nanny. Karla was disappointed because she had liked the arrangement, but went along with Stephen's wishes. She wasn't prepared to give up her career to stay home, which was another attitude that brought disapproval from many people, including the pediatrician.

Karla and Stephen had to ignore advice from everyone and do what was right for them. Even more important, they had to define what manhood and womanhood means to them. In that particular area, almost no one is without an opinion. Being a hairdresser isn't masculine enough for some people; being a pilot isn't feminine enough for others. Even amidst the gender role shake-up that we've all been part of, there are those who will criticize any decision involving role reversals that are the least bit nontraditional.

Let It Be

When we talk about making decisions, it might seem that the opposite could be called indecision. And to many people, indecision means weakness. But aren't there times when not deciding ends up being the best choice?

Libby's grown children and her friends urged her to marry Dan. "At your age, you won't have many more chances," they all said. "He's so good looking, someone will grab him up," one sage told her. At fifty-two, Libby knew that her choices in men weren't going to blossom like apples on a tree. Dan was handsome, charming, and no doubt met other women when he traveled for his company. Still, Libby liked to come home to her own place and do as she pleased. Her privacy was extremely important to her. And, although she didn't tell anyone, Libby didn't really like Dan's children very much. If she married him, she'd no doubt have to spend more time with his family. Frankly, she liked everything the way it was.

Yet Libby's indecision was driving her crazy. It was as if she saw only two choices: don't marry and lose Dan, or marry and lose her freedom. As time went on, she recognized that another option was to keep things just the same. Later, if other events intervened, she could open up the decision-making process again.

Fred couldn't decide whether or not to leave his job, although his family kept telling him that it was a dead-end position. All this advice was making Fred anxious. One day, he sat by himself and thought about his choices, one of which was to put off the decision until he was ready to make it. Once he realized he could simply put the issue on hold for a while, his anxiety immediately lessened.

Perhaps you have felt pressure to make a decision—now! But how critical is the situation? Must it be resolved today? Tomorrow? Perhaps you can consider that, for now, you're not to make this decision at all.

LISTEN AND LEARN

When you examine your own attitudes and beliefs, and listen to your own gut feelings, you may still find yourself afraid of the consequences of going with your instincts but against conventional wisdom. You may be afraid of making a mistake, being ridiculed, or even being disliked. Of course, these things can happen even when you make a choice that others approve of. If a decision doesn't work out, they'll forget that they applauded your choice and start giving you more of their good advice, now that you need new direction.

In some situations, you can help lessen your fear if you gather as much information as possible. Go ahead, ask your usual confidants and go to the experts, too. Get as many views as you can. Find others who have made a similar choice and ask about the results of their decisions. True, you will probably find many different outcomes, but that's okay. You'll learn a lot in the process.

For example, Arthur and Tami learned about the challenges of interfaith marriage by talking to those who had already faced this issue. They heard about problems, but they also heard about the special beauty that can come from respecting two faiths in one household. Likewise, Arthur heard stories about parents who never did accept such marriages. In some cases, the marriage ended in divorce; in others, it added an element of challenge—the "we'll prove you wrong" attitude was often strong in interfaith relationships. By the way, this isn't always a negative element. Despite conventional wisdom, I've seen cases in which people will fight harder to maintain a relationship, or succeed in a particular career, because others were so convinced it would never work out.

Always think about the motives others have for giving advice. Is their concern genuine, or could there be an element of jealousy or resentment hidden behind their words? Someone who tells you not to take a risk may be envious of your ability to do so. For instance, a person who tells you not to bother writing a novel or pursuing a graduate degree may be threatened by your willingness to try something difficult. This was Nan's husband's problem. He was threatened by her willingness to work at her art projects when there was no assurance that anyone would care to look at them, let alone buy them. He didn't have that kind of commitment to a challenge.

Examine Your Choices Anew

One reason making decisions can be especially difficult today is that we have more freedom to choose our own destiny. Additionally, we live at a time when the world is changing so rapidly that we are bombarded by messages of constantly changing ethics and morality. Movie stars, media personalities, this or that politician, new schools of thought in medicine or psychology all have *the* "answers." But many times their solutions conflict with one another, and they may even conflict with what we were taught as children.

In order to make choices from our own gut instinct, we must rethink our beliefs. We may choose to keep our old stereotypes about what is right and wrong, or we may choose to change our beliefs. To be sure, there is no need to throw out everything we've been taught just because it sounds old-fashioned. By the same token, we can get rid of useless old ideas and let in new, more useful ones. The happiest people I know are those who remain thoughtfully flexible. They don't mindlessly follow every new fad, but they are open to new ideas and aren't afraid to alter their beliefs if conditions warrant doing so.

In the old world, many people believed that it was *always* right to fight for one's country. Some people followed that belief with blind devotion—witness Nazi Germany. In our own country, many young men decided it was wrong to fight in the Vietnam War. The "right" decision in one situation became the "wrong" decision in another. Some young men went to jail or left the country because they believed strongly that it was an immoral war. As the war dragged on, many people began to agree that this was no longer a black and white issue.

Years ago, it was shocking to see young people living together. If a couple was having a sexual relationship, it was carried out in secret. Ironically, I've talked to many grandparents who are reassuring their children that the unmarried grandchild who lives with a partner seems just fine. Similarly, I've talked with a few grandparents who are more accepting of a grandchild's homosexuality than the parents are. We might say that these older people are able to take a very long view of life.

Are there situations in your life where you've thrown out an old attitude but now you wish you hadn't—or maybe you've clung to an old standard that doesn't work anymore? You may find this in family relationships, your work life, your political views, or your spiritual life. Take a look at the process you went through when you chose to change, or maintain, a value or attitude. You'll learn much about yourself when you examine how you made your decision.

THE SLIPPERY SLOPE OF AUTHORITY

All my life, I have watched Jewish couples stand under the traditional wedding canopy and seen many a young groom break a wine glass. When I was a child, my rabbi told me that the broken glass symbolized the destruction of the ancient Jewish temple. I believed him, of course, because he was a powerful authority figure. Years later, another rabbi said that the glass symbolized how fragile marriage can be. I've since heard other explanations, all delivered with the weight of authority.

This simple example is typical of life today: We face many experts with conflicting advice. One expert told Jack that he must reject his homosexuality or he would never be emotionally well. Jack found that impossible to do and was relieved when another expert told him that what he really needed was help in accepting who he is. One set of experts told Jack's parents that they were responsible for their son's lifestyle; another set of experts said that was nonsense and encouraged them to accept Jack's homosexuality as biologically predetermined. Both sets of experts cited studies to back up their claims.

We all get excited when studies "prove" that what we believe is right and we're angry with research that disproves our beliefs. Furthermore, what one study claims today is shown to be false by new research released tomorrow. A medication I was on years ago has now been taken off the market because new studies demonstrated that it is dangerous. We also see situations in which a second or even third opinion may negate the need for surgery that the first doctor emphatically recommended. We can say only one thing for sure: Experts and various authorities are fallible, and we should feel free to challenge their advice.

If you have ever been in therapy you may have been given advice that doesn't feel right to you. But, you think, a professional advised the course of action, so it must be right. Not so. Get other opinions, think about the reasons for your reluctance. Go with your own gut instincts.

I'm not suggesting that we disregard the expertise of others. But I am suggesting that we learn to be partners with the experts whose counsel we seek. If you have a difficult time challenging authority, enlist the support of someone who will help you—talk to your doctor or the school psychologist or whomever. You may be able to find alternate ways to solve your problem. You may have more options than you think. Furthermore, a sincere and trustworthy expert should not fear a request for a second opinion or be threatened by your questions and concerns. If he or she tries to intimidate you or makes fun of you in any way, then this expert is not worthy of your trust. Move on.

Subtle Poison

Ed had a long-standing dream of opening his own business. To many of us this sounds like a reasonable goal, but to his family, it was a joke. A joke. They laughed and teased him and told him he didn't have what it takes to be an entrepreneur. For years Ed continued to listen to this talk that poisoned his dream.

After earning many promotions at a small company, Ed began to realize that his boss and coworkers saw him as a very capable person. In fact, the only time Ed didn't feel capable was in the midst of his large family. Ed attended a seminar for aspiring entrepreneurs and heard the facilitator encourage the participants to turn their dreams into reachable goals. More importantly, the woman warned them about paying too much attention to family and friends who could poison dreams with their negativity. This sent a shiver through Ed—it was as if she knew his family.

For two years Ed quietly planned his move, but he never told his family about his new business venture until it actually happened. In the meantime, he met new people in a business network. These men and women didn't have an ounce of negativity in them. Rather than tearing him down, they supported him in his quest.

For some people, it's necessary to stay away from those who are overly critical and negative, even if they are your family. It's possible, however, that a confrontation will remedy the situation and family members will curtail their hurtful talk. Unfortunately, this isn't always an option.

The trouble with this poison is that it doesn't always kill immediately. It can be diluted so it eats away at the spirit slowly but surely. Negativity can cause you to doubt yourself and your own best judgments. This is especially true when the messages of doom and gloom come from those you love.

Here are some of the common negative beliefs that can poison a person's life:

- You're over forty now, you've missed your chance to get married. Just accept it and you'll be happier.
- You're too old to go to graduate school. At your age, you'll never keep up with the younger people.
- No one can make a living _____ (*fill in the blank:* painting, acting, composing, writing, making custom clothing, reading Tarot cards at parties, being a professional clown, baking wedding cakes, and so on.)
- Your child will turn out rotten if you go back to work.

- Men only like tall, thin women.
- Women don't like bald men.
- If you succeed, you'll lose your husband.
- If you don't succeed, you'll lose your wife.

Now this is just a sampling of the kinds of messages that people are poisoned with. You might look at many of these statements and think, "Why would anyone say something that stupid?" But the woman who makes a great living reading Tarot cards at parties is just as real as the man who lost all his hair at age thirty and spent many lonely hours convinced that no woman would ever want him. In both cases, well-meaning older siblings had tried to "protect" these two people, but instead, they used the vestiges of childhood authority to discourage the desire for a particular career in one case, and a mate in the other.

You may not be able to eliminate all the negative influences in your life, but you can keep these voices from penetrating your consciousness. Moreover, you can examine the motives for this slow, steady poisoning of your ideas. You may find that these people project their own fears on to you, or, you may notice that they don't yet know that you've grown up and have your own attitudes.

Stretch and Expand

You may choose to see Uncle Oscar, who always puts you down, at the annual Thanksgiving gathering. However, you don't have to limit yourself to his lousy company. If you are surrounded by negative voices, make some new friends. Ed found a support system by going to a seminar for entrepreneurs; Barbara, a wedding cake caterer, joined a women's business group where members were encouraged to strike out on their own.

As you broaden your horizons and mingle with many different kinds of people, you'll find that there are myriad attitudes and belief systems in the world. One client's political volunteer work enabled her to create a rich, fulfilling life that her mother had predicted would never be possible until she lost weight. This woman was almost thirty-five before she went out on her own and began to build a life independent from her single mother. Only when she was living the life she deserved was she able to address the weight problem that had been affecting her self-esteem.

Sometimes the people around you will notice the changes you are making and be happy for you. They may even change themselves and adopt new attitudes. But you can't count on it, and you most certainly can't force it. If this positive result occurs, it usually happens by itself.

Live Your Decision Before You Make It

It isn't always possible to experiment before plunging in, but sometimes it can help you make your choice. Let's say, for example, that a man wants to marry you, but you aren't sure you're in love. Spend as much time as possible experiencing his lifestyle and imagining what it would be like to be married to him. Don't make the decision until you've weighed all options, because dating and marriage are two different things. One of my clients balked at the suggestion she spend more time with a man who was interested in her and talking about marriage. That realization alone nudged her to make a decision not to marry him—if she didn't look forward to spending more time with him, then why would she want to commit her whole life to him in marriage?

Perhaps you're considering a career change. But you're afraid you won't like a new field, or perhaps you aren't sure you can adjust to something so different. Why not do some research and learn all you can about the *reality* of the new field? Maybe it's almost as good as your fantasies, but you'll never know until you do the work to find out. Perhaps you could do some volunteer work in the field or consider a trial period in a new job. You may have more options than you know.

Over the years, many of my clients have talked about their desires to relocate to a new area of the country. Usually this urge stays vague until they begin to imagine themselves in the new place. Doubts begin to crop up when they wonder how they will make new friends or become involved in the community. When I've suggested that they subscribe to the local newspaper or find out if organizations they belong to have chapters in the new location, they often look startled because they've never thought of doing that kind of practical footwork. And while some clients have decided against a town or city after learning more about it, others stopped procrastinating and enthusiastically made the decision to move.

Mistake or Calamity?

No one has all the answers and there is no such thing as a completely risk-free decision. There will always be consequences when you decide to marry or divorce or change jobs. Some consequences might be trivial and you wonder what all the fuss was about. For example, you take up flower arranging only to discover that it bores you tears—just as Aunt Addie said it would. So what? You tried it and didn't like it.

There are many adages that express the same encouraging idea:

- Successful people make the most mistakes because they try more new things.
- The only people who haven't failed are those who never try anything.
- The batter with the most home runs usually strikes out a lot too.
- We learn more from our failures than from our successes.

These observations are usually true. Most of the time, a mistake can be considered a lesson learned, or a temporary set-back, or something we needed to do in order to satisfy a curiosity. Few mistakes are calamities that can't be reversed.

WHAT'S THE WORST THING THAT COULD HAPPEN?

You're closing in on a major decision, but you can't quite get there. When this happens, fear is usually rearing its head. So face the fear and ask, "If I do this, what's the worst thing that could happen if it turns out to be the wrong choice?" You will usually find that the worst thing is not so terrible. Ask yourself if your family will stop talking to you if you take that job as a bartender? Will your friends turn away from you if you marry the rich woman they say is so wrong for you? What will happen if you quit your job and head for the country?

Most of the time these decisions can be undone. Sure, it's harder to get divorced than it is to change jobs, but it's possible. If your heart is telling you that this woman is right for you, then listen carefully to your head and that rapidly beating heart. (There are a few cases in which friends and relatives do see things you don't, and their advice can keep you out of danger. For example, a client who wanted to marry a drug addict with the hope of changing him, could have put herself in jeopardy. However, most of the time, advice from others is based on a far less factual foundation.)

My client who wanted to be a bartender while she went to college was bucking her family value system, which allowed the women to have only "respectable" jobs. But Cora liked the odd hours. She was a night person and didn't enjoy office work. That decision was right for her, but it wasn't until she got her degree that her family stopped criticizing her for her "low-life" job.

Had Cora identified herself with the "good girl" syndrome, she might have given up her own desire for an off-beat job. Examine your own need for approval. Do you sometimes do things because you'll be viewed as a "bad boy" or a "bad girl" if you don't? Whose approval are you seeking? Why do you need it?

Granted, it's possible that the worst will happen, but few things in life can't be mended. If you don't succeed, the experience you had may be enough to teach you to avoid the same mistake in the future. If we live in a thoughtful way, we can learn from our mistakes, and in fact, we may learn that a so-called incorrect action was merely a stepping stone to something else. Some people simply refuse to acknowledge that there is such a thing as a mistake—they simply call them "nonsuccesses." Make up your own mind and use the language you agree with, because if you don't consider your options, make decisions, and take action, your life will be dull indeed.

Add a Time Limit

Let's say you want to be an actress, but everyone around you is discouraging you from taking such a big risk: "What about security, stability, and reality? Give up your pipe dream and get on with a regular life." Perhaps these voices are in your head, too. When I have clients who are in this kind of dilemma, I often suggest that they put a time limit on their decision.

For example, the aspiring actress could make a plan to get started in the field—taking classes, assembling portfolios, working in community theater, and so on. Then she could give herself one, two, three, or whatever number of years, seems right to achieve her own definition of success. Would she need to have landed two parts, ten roles, or even one television modeling spot in order to believe that progress had been made? After the time limit is up, she can evaluate her success and decide what to do at that point. Some people will decide to move on and find another career; others would persevere; still others may modify the plan to accommodate both security and the dream.

Time limits can work in other ways as well. For example, if you've spent years involved in yo-yo dieting, you could say, "I'm not going to diet for a year. I'm going to be as happy as I can be and take all this pressure off." Or, perhaps you are having sexual problems and you aren't ready to talk with your partner about

1. You could say, "I will fake orgasms for six weeks and see it feels." After six weeks you may have learned some things about yourself and perhaps about your partner as well. You can then make a different decision if you want to. One client said, "I will not visit my mother, who gives me a few zinging put-downs every time I see her, for two months. Then I'll decide what to do about the way she treats me. But for two months, I'll be free of her nasty tongue."

Feeling Guilty? So What?

Guilt is an emotion that we all experience from time to time. Buying a dress you can't afford might make you feel guilty, but it also makes you feel young and sexy—and maybe young and sexy won out that day. So what if you feel a little guilty? It's not such a big thing. The next time you see a dress that costs too much, the guilt about spending money that's really needed for something else will probably be stronger than the appeal of the dress.

We're often put in a position to make decisions that have conflicting feelings attached to them. We plan a vacation with our partner, but the kids complain about being left out. We go anyway, because maybe having time alone with our partner is important enough to endure a little guilt. So we just do it anyway.

Confused? Try a Different Tack

Sometimes the opposite approach is worth trying. For example, a woman with an extremely demanding mother eventually decided to bend over backward to please her. But even then, whatever she did still wasn't good enough. What an eye-opening experience that was! Learning that she could never please her mother, she decided to give up trying and began to set limits on the time she spent visiting this unpleasant woman.

I've seen this work again and again. Many of us need to prove to ourselves that a certain behavior simply won't keep the peace or make everything okay in our relationships.

Do It Any Way You Can

Don't wait to conquer all your fears. You may never need to face them all—especially if you just forge ahead in spite of them. For instance, if you want to travel but are afraid to fly, drive or take the bus. If you're afraid to tell off your busy-body cousin, write a letter instead. A woman I know was afraid of making speeches, but she found that having a glass of wine before "show time" relaxed her. Sure, maybe the perfect solution would be to conquer the fear, but this worked for her at the time. Others might call taking a bus instead of a plane the "wrong" way to travel, but so what? If you're happy, what difference does it make what others think? Maybe one day you'll be ready to address some of your fears, but in the meantime, you can still be happy.

Get Help

Sometimes we're simply unable to make changes by ourselves, but we're afraid to admit it for fear of looking weak. For many people the "right" thing is to be completely independent, never asking others for help. However, all of us need other people in our lives and true intimacy comes from sharing our thoughts and feelings with others. For some people, a support group is a good place to work on changing things in their lives. Others seek professional counseling and find a peer group to work with too. Sometimes a new friend can be your shoulder to lean on while you consider a decision. There are many sources of support and help.

While I caution you not to rely too much on others when you are making decisions, it makes sense to find constructive help, especially if you are severely troubled by situations in your life. Seeking help can be a positive step toward learning to make your own decisions in your own unique way.

Marriage, family, sex, careers, planning weddings, getting divorces, dating, raising children, choosing homes and clothes and cars, taking vacations, finding friends, practicing your religion, working for your causes, and managing money are what I refer to collectively as the "stuff of life." We spend most of our time involved in the day-to-day details of living. And these are areas in which we often need to examine options, choose from among a number of good choices, and then make the best of the results, at least until we decide to choose again.

In the next chapters, we'll take a look at some major and minor decisions that individuals made about the stuff of life. I encourage you to look at each story as a possible scenario in your own life. What would you do? How do you react to the people involved? Frankly, you may not like all the people or their decisions, although I think most of the characters in these true stories will seem much like you or someone you know. As you read, gain some practice in making your own decisions by examining what you would or would not do if faced with a similar dilemma.

Four

Love, Marriage, and Divorce

When I was a young girl there were few choices about marriage—at least that's what I was taught. Being born female meant getting married when you were grown up, having children, and then waiting for grandchildren. Education, while important, was not as significant as the "big event" of marriage. Unmarried women were called, horror of horrors, "old maids."

Young men had to get an education, of course, because they were expected to be breadwinners. That meant being ambitious and hard driving in order to be a good provider and be considered a "good catch" by young women's families. When men didn't marry they were accused of being "playboys." (Given the terms attached to single men and women, it's no wonder marriage seemed mandatory for women.)

Women also were told that they could never say no to their husbands (even some religious teachings tried to justify this attitude), his needs came first, and if he had affairs you were supposed to ignore them. (Women were not supposed to have affairs and were considered tramps if they did.) In the world I grew up in you were lucky if you were happy, but if you weren't, you had to make the best of it anyway. Divorce was out of the question.

If this sounds odd, believe me when I say that these were the rules I was taught by my mother, and the rules I watched my parents live by. I know that I'm not alone. When a friend of mine was fifty-six, she called her parents and told them that her husband of thirty-five years was in love with a woman half his age. Her mother's response? "You have to make the marriage work. Just do it." In her mother's world, and my family's world, too, divorce was a terrible failure. My friend's mother would have preferred a sham marriage for her daughter over the "shame" of divorce.

BRAVO FOR NEW ATTITUDES

Thankfully, these attitudes are no longer so prevalent, in part because many in my generation have made an effort to erase the mental tapes that are filled with rigid rules. They are replacing the old messages with ones that emphasize choice, personal responsibility, internal integrity, and freedom. For example, I taught both my daughters and my son that marriage is optional. Sure, it can be wonderful, and I'm glad I made that choice. But there are other options. I certainly don't want my children to be unhappily married, rather than content and single just to satisfy a societal expectation. Furthermore, they are free to live with their partners before marriage, or in lieu of it. And while I am happy that I have some terrific grandchildren, I have known all along that my children's purpose in life was not to make me a grandmother. (You'd be surprised how many parents believe that their children owe them grandchildren.)

In addition to greater freedom to choose or reject marriage, men and women now also have more options about their roles within relationships. Of course, women and men are inundated with advice about how to interact, but one thing is absolute—there simply is no one way to live, communicate, make love, raise children, do housework, create a social life, make a living, or even separate or get divorced.

Over the years, I've worked with individuals and couples who represent a variety of attitudes and expectations and who made very different choices about their relationships. From working with people who have very different personalities, I've discovered that relationship problems often stem from an unwillingness or inability to break out of old patterns and expectations. Sometimes this unhappiness is based on trying to fit into a mold that appears socially acceptable to others, especially family members. In other words, even with all the freedom available to us, conventional wisdom and popular opinion still can have enormous influence on our choices. But I've learned that for every one hundred people there are one hundred—or more—right answers. Let's look at some of these relationships to get a glimpse of how they work—or don't work.

IT'S OKAY TO SETTLE

Mary thought about divorce a lot—almost every day. She enjoyed so many things about her life, including her home, her friends, her children, and her part-time job. Trouble was, she didn't particularly enjoy her husband, Harold. Naturally, divorce seemed like a good idea, at least some of the time.

Mary talked with her friend, Jean, who had been divorced for several years. Jean was very bitter because she had once lived in a beautiful big house, had household help, took fabulous vacations, and had just about anything else money could buy. After her divorce, Jean had far less money to live on—by her standards, it was barely enough. So she was angry and embittered, because those material things had been very important to her.

Whenever Mary talked to Jean, she realized that she would be in a similar situation if she chose divorce. She might even end up worse off than Jean. Mary allowed herself a secret visit to a lawyer to assess her situation, and spent months seriously considering a divorce, but ultimately, she closed the door on the idea.

Mary was certain she would be accused of "settling" for a mediocre marriage. Other good friends had long wondered why she didn't divorce Harold—after all, she and her husband had nothing in common. Mary had always managed to keep the time she spent with Harold to a minimum, and once she reached her decision to stay, she viewed her interaction with him as a small price to pay for continuing her secure life.

For many people, Mary's decision would be absolutely wrong. I can hear the cries of protest: She's shallow, she's too afraid to strike out on her own, she's selling herself short, she's cheating her husband out of a better life, she's behaving like a prostitute. But I've come to believe that there are many people like Mary, people who are no longer content in their marriages, but who also believe that divorce is not always the right answer. Yes, they make the necessary tradeoffs and compromises, and then vow to make the best of their situations. While I can't always agree with their decision to stay, I can't fault them for it, either, especially if they have approached their choice with intelligence and an open mind. And, I've also worked with many divorced people who wish they had considered all the ramifications before they made the choice to end their marriage—because divorced life isn't always easy street.

Is it society's dirty little secret that many long-married people are unhappy? I can't count the number of women who are tired—tired of *his* moodiness, *his* demands, *his* sloppiness, *his* television programs. And while men have their complaints and disappointments too, studies have established that marriage is generally more beneficial for men than it is for women. Traditional roles have usually fulfilled men's physical and emotional needs, but sometimes at the expense of women's needs.

As a group, married men report being happier than married women; single women, as a group, report being happier than single men. In other words, the way marriage has been structured, it meets men's needs more than it meets women's. In addition, many men feel great autonomy within marriage; once their basic needs are met, they are free to seek personal satisfaction in work, friendships, hobbies, and so forth. Women, on the other hand, often believe they must subordinate their needs to those of their family.

The experiences of others can help us make our decisions about staying in marriages or even getting married in the first place. Nowadays, when people see what the possibilities are, they may find that they can create more equal relationships, ones that meet everyone's needs. Let's explore some situations that can give us the range of options available.

I Did the Right Thing, or Did I?

Pearl is proud that she's been such a good wife. She tells me that she took good care of her children and her husband, *always* putting their needs ahead of her own. She brags about the fact that she never refused to have sex with her husband, even though she didn't care much about it herself. She even stood by her man when he was fooling around with a woman at work. Actually, Matt had given her everything she wanted—unless he thought it wasn't good for her. "No one can blame me for anything," she said. "I did the right thing all my life."

Yet when sixty-five-year old Pearl started to feel more comfortable with me, the real story began to emerge. Matt was abusive—not physically—but verbally and emotionally. He was cold and distant, except when he wanted sex. The rest of the time, he belittled her. Finally, Pearl admitted, "If I had it to do over again, I'd have left. I wouldn't have wasted my life catering to a selfish man. My mistake was being too dependent. Even my children encouraged me to go back to school so I could make a living and leave if I chose to. But I didn't listen, and now it's too late."

Pearl is grateful for one thing. While she never openly supported the women's movement, and in fact, condemned it early on, she knows that life can be different for her daughters and her grandchildren. No longer physically strong enough to make a different choice, Pearl still caters to her husband because she can't stand the fights if she doesn't. Pearl believes that she may have done the right thing according to her mother's standards, but she is now left with little except a basket full of regrets.

I think it's important for a woman like Mary to hear about women like Pearl. Sure, settling for a mediocre marriage is a valid choice, but the specter of missed chances and a future of regret must be faced too. For now, Pearl believes she is stuck. Mary doesn't feel stuck—yet. And Mary hasn't made her decision forever. It's possible she will change her mind next year or even ten years from now. Of course, it's also possible that her husband will one day call it quits; women who choose to settle must consider how they will cope if this happens. But, the most important principle for Mary to remember: No one is forced to stick to a decision that he or she later regrets.

TEMPORARY CHOICES

Sometimes a decision just can't be made right now. For example, I've counseled some couples who are miserable in their marriages, but don't want to get a divorce. After months of working with them but making little progress, I often suggest my "caring roommate" intervention as a last option before separation. Simply put, this process calls a halt to still more attempts to patch the marriage; instead, the couple temporarily lives together as roommates would. They must be considerate toward each other, much the way they were when they were young adults sharing apartments with same-sex housemates. The arrangement is one of convenience, not a commitment to love. In order for this to work, they must agree that their personal lives are their own.

What is the purpose of this intervention? I have found that men and women are able to drop their anger and hostility when they no longer focus on what is expected of them as husbands and wives. When they stop worrying about what they are supposed to feel as a marriage partner and how they are supposed to behave in that role, they may be able to relate to each other as friends. I've observed the following results:

1. Some couples became closer when they worked on issues from a different point of view—as friends, not spouses. They began to see each other as individuals, not *my* husband or *my* wife. Most of these couples chose to stay married and were able to make the adjustment back to the love commitment, but without losing the ability to be friends.
2. Some couples decide they like the new freedom and choose to separate, but on friendly terms. Vindictiveness rarely enters the divorce climate in these situations.
3. Some couples couldn't handle this arrangement and chose to continue their disastrous course of fights and conflict.
4. So far, only one couple decided to remain friendly roommates on a permanent basis. This couple liked each other as friends, and also liked the idea of saving the money that a divorce would cost. This arrangement has been going on for only three years and either partner could opt to change it at any time. So in this context, permanent simply means ongoing for now.

I believe strongly in using this technique for troubled marriages because as couples relate in a new way, they are usually able to let go of their old conventional ideas about marriage. Just imagine if everyone treated their marriage partner with the same respect they once treated their roommates. Maybe it's this realization that makes the technique work.

If you and your spouse find yourself in a rocky spot, consider giving this "roommate" solution a try. It could work for you as it has for others. And remember, you don't have to tell the world about it. Some couples have discovered that if they blab, blab, blab about their arrangement with friends and family, all they get back is criticism. Here, as in so many other situations, keep your own counsel.

To Fight or Not to Fight

Go ahead, let off steam, get what's bothering you off your chest—a good fight clears the air. So goes much of the advice we hear. But I've seen couples who gain little or nothing by this counsel. For example, Mary, who chose to stay in her mediocre marriage believes there is little to gain by airing her feelings. She's tried it and confrontation simply doesn't work. She can't change her husband's mind about anything, and she prefers to say "yes, yes, yes," and then do her own thing anyway. Granted, not everyone would care to live like this, but doing battle over principle just doesn't interest Mary.

Another myth that's passed from one generation to another: Never go to bed angry—always solve the problem and make up before the night is over. Sure, this might work for some people. But it's equally true that sleeping on a problem might be a better solution, because we often see issues much differently in the morning.

We also don't necessarily need to fight on the spot, so to speak. Many times it's better to let something go, consider it, and then return to the issue at another time. After all, some conflicts are not going to be settled all at once. There are times in every marriage when we must agree to disagree. Democrats married to Republicans often find themselves in this situation. I know a couple who have never voted for the same political candidates, and for twenty years they've agreed to disagree. If they hadn't come to this arrangement, their marriage would have been one long argument.

There are some couples who seem to settle almost every disagreement in a peaceful manner—no shouting, no turned backs, no slammed doors, no silent treatment. They don't even have to haggle or negotiate much. Conventional wisdom tells us that there must be something deeply wrong in the relationship. I've heard professionals claim that where there is no rancor or anger, there is no love. This simply isn't true. Is it so difficult to believe that some people can solve a problem without fighting and yelling? Perhaps these are the people we should be studying and learning from.

MUTUAL CONVENIENCE

Some situations are best resolved by a "convenience" decision. For example, there are marriages that are kept intact in such a way as to serve the needs of both partners; these relationships are mutually agreed upon arrangements of convenience.

For many years Betty suffered because of Mark's sexual indifference. She also was shocked and uncomfortable when he encouraged her to have affairs to satisfy her sexual needs. But finally, the truth came out. Mark thought Betty was one of the most wonderful people he had ever known. But he wasn't attracted to her because he's gay.

Heartache and anger inevitably followed, but gradually the couple began to relate to each other in a new way. They decided to stay married and live separate romantic lives. For now, they believe this is the best arrangement for their nearly grown children. They have told their son and daughter the truth, but they haven't told anyone else. Eventually they may have to make a different choice, but for now, they see no reason to disrupt a household when they are making it work. This solution would be odd to some people, but I believe Betty and Mark are following their hearts and their heads.

Betty and Mark are certainly not alone. There are probably millions of people who have lived with this secret. Fortunately, gay people are no longer under the same kind of pressure to keep their sexual orientation a secret. Most are not entering heterosexual marriages in vain attempts to be "normal."

Patrick and Edith are in their seventies and they have decided to marry and take care of each other in their older years. Sharing expenses and chores for one household makes life easier for both of them and they each have more money to spend on trips and clothes. While not romantically involved, they are fond friends and very devoted to each other.

Some older couples live this way, but don't get married because they don't want to lose the financial benefits they receive by staying single. Patrick and Edith were well off financially and didn't mind a slight cut in income. Either way, these convenience marriages might be more common than we think. (This is not to say that all marriages between older people are based on convenience. I know of many that are romantic and sexy. All I'm saying here is that convenience arrangements are valid too.)

Convenience marriages follow a wide variety of patterns. Take the Wilsons. They married several years ago because they both had several children and wanted a big house to raise them in. Combining their income (with a formal agreement) was the motivation for the union. So far, it seems to have worked.

Sue and Bart are in their thirties and sick of being single. Both want children, and while not wildly in love with each other, they have comfortably drifted into a marriage for the purpose of raising a family. Few of their friends or family members understand them. But I'm wondering if Sue and Bart will eventually grow to love one another. Across the world, millions of men and women enter into marriages arranged by their parents. Many of these couples eventually come to love each other deeply. As I talked with them, I could see the possibility for romance, perhaps because Sue and Bart started with great mutual respect and an easy friendship.

Few therapists would recommend marriages of convenience. However, to say they are always wrong is a mistake too. For the couples above, the wrong thing is right, and I've noted over the years that some of these convenience marriages are happier than many conventional ones—you know, the ones driven by wild passion and being "crazy in love." But when the fire burned out, there was little left but a pile of ashes.

DOLLAR SIGNS PREVAIL

Melissa came to counseling with an interesting dilemma. She was engaged to Bruce, an attractive, attentive man who was madly in love with her. Melissa was sure she would marry Bruce, but she wanted to sort out some guilt feelings. As she put it, "I've married twice for love, and this time I'm marrying for money."

As her story unfolded, I understood Melissa's desire for some security. The first time, she'd married her high school boyfriend, who'd had a drinking problem. After a few episodes of physical abuse, she took her infant daughter and went home to her parents. The second time Melissa married, she was twenty-six and Roger seemed like the perfect partner. He was older and settled, and didn't have troublesome addictions, at least not obvious ones. This marriage lasted eleven years. After his first affair, she took him back because she loved him and he seemed so penitent. After the second affair, she was beginning to wonder about his need to confess his infidelities. By the third affair, love had turned to hate and Melissa's second marriage was history.

Now, a mother of three, Melissa had struggled on her own for four years, making ends meet on minimal child support and her salary as a secretary. Enter Bruce. Kind to the children, generous to Melissa, Bruce seemed like a dream come true. But Melissa was honest enough to admit that if he'd been financially strapped or stingy, she never would have become involved with him.

After much soul searching, Melissa faced all the negative aspects of marrying for money, but she went ahead anyway. I respected her need to evaluate her decision and I respected her choice to go ahead with the wedding. Her maturity was such that she knew she was not getting guarantees and she certainly wasn't experiencing the so-called "bells and whistles" of romance. But the bells and whistles hadn't brought her happiness and she was no longer impressed with them. A year into her marriage to Bruce, Melissa told me that she was thrilled with the way it was working out. She had turned out to be a very good wife to a man who liked nothing better than doting on her and her children.

Tightwad Tony

Poor Ann thought she'd be wealthy Ann. At fifty-two, she'd been wined and dined for a year by Tony, age sixty. He had never married before, but he wanted to marry Ann. He also wanted a prenuptial agreement that made it clear that his siblings and nieces and nephews were going to share in his wealth. Ann wasn't concerned; there was plenty of money to go around. And he had promised to give her whatever she wanted and provide for her if he died.

Ann thought she went into the marriage with her eyes open, but they might as well have been closed. Marrying for money was a big mistake, because once the honeymoon was over, Tony turned into the cheapest man that ever lived. As the truth became known, Ann learned that even Tony's brothers and sisters had complained for years about his miserliness. Furthermore, he wasn't generous to Ann in his will, and most of the money was slated to go to the nieces and nephews. Ann ended up in a situation that was intolerable. She barely had a dollar in her pocket and she'd quit her job to live the "high life" with Tony.

For Ann, marrying for money was a huge mistake. The "wrong" thing really was wrong. But lavish courtship had blinded her to the reality. When she looked back, Ann could recognize signs of the stingy Tony she would come to know—the smaller than necessary apartment, the older car, the minimal tips he left. At the time, she thought he was just being tasteful and not showing off his wealth.

Some men marry for money, too. I've known women who were

aware of this when they married a younger, handsome, broke man, but they decided that going for some excitement and romance was worth it. Some of these marriages worked and some didn't. But I can say the same for the more conventional partnerships I've seen. The same is true for those who marry a wealthy spouse but also continue to make their own money. For many women and men, a career is at least as important as money, and they want to have their own accomplishments as well as the financial security the other partner brings.

My only advice about the issue of marrying for money is to be certain you know what you're doing. Sure, listen to others' opinions, especially if you are wavering or have some reservations. If Ann had listened to her gut, she might have made a different choice. Melissa did listen to her gut—it was her head that raised the doubts. Ultimately, you'll make your own decision, but think long and hard before doing so. You could be a Melissa—or you could be an Ann.

SURVIVING COMMON MARRIAGE MYTHS

Lauren and Allen agreed on almost everything, but they were in trouble after only two years of marriage. "We don't spend enough time together," Lauren said. "When we're not working, I want to do things together. After all, why get married if you don't spend your free time with each other? All he wants to do is play cards and watch sports on television with his friends. Now he tells me to go out with my friends and get some interests of my own. And he doesn't even want to listen to me talk about my troubles at work or about problems with my mother. This isn't what marriage is supposed to be."

Allen claims he was never much of a talker and what he really wants is to relax and watch movies and sports when he's home.

He doesn't care to discuss his own work problems, much less Lauren's. "She has other friends she can talk to about those things," he said.

From the outside, I'm sure that Allen seemed like the perfect husband. Before they were married, he and Lauren worked out a detailed division of household chores; they have both joint and individual checking and savings accounts, and money conflicts were conspicuous only by their absence. According to Lauren, Allen was a great lover who satisfied her need for frequent and intense sex. He liked to go shopping for pretty lingerie, and when it was his turn to cook he often put candles and flowers on the table. But he wasn't her best friend, and this threatened their relationship.

Unfortunately, I've seen many couples like Lauren and Allen. One partner's expectations are usually too high and he or she just can't stop wanting to share everything with the marriage partner. Some people think that the only valid marriage is one in which the partners are "best friends," however they define that. Being good or best friends is nice when it works and when it is what both people want. But this isn't always possible or even desirable.

Lauren had believed the myth that goes something like this: If he really loved me he'd want to be with me all the time, every free minute. Or, if she loved me, she wouldn't want to talk on the phone with her friends or go shopping with her sister—she'd want to be with me every evening.

Whew! What a tall order for any one human being to fill. Be all things to your partner—friend, confidant, lover, mother/father, provider, nurturer, constant companion for movies and bowling. Of course it's natural that partners try to be friends as well as lovers—that's what attracts them in the first place. But separate interests and spending time with other people—or alone—can usually result in a more harmonious relationship.

When Lauren realized that Allen wasn't ever going to be much help with her problems at work, she took the pressure off. That was her first step. Besides, her women friends understood her and, she admitted, it was much more satisfying to talk with them. It was her expectation that Allen *should* want to listen that had caused the problem.

Because Allen and Lauren were so compatible in other ways, they straightened out their problems in only a few sessions. Allen agreed to be more attentive some of the time, and Lauren agreed to take the pressure off and resume some interests that she had dropped when they married. (She thought she had to drop these activities because he didn't share them.) Lauren began to take classes at the local community college two nights a week and she often studied while Allen watched his games on television. Both were much happier.

Joined Hearts or Joined Hips

I have concluded that each person in a relationship is more content when there is ample opportunity to develop his or her potential, experience separate interests, and have some outside friendships. Togetherness is great, but too much can wear out both partners. Sooner or later one person becomes resentful about being pulled away from other interests. Most people are more content in marriages in which time together is balanced by time away. They often find that their time spent as companions is richer and more precious when both partners are living full, active lives.

It isn't always the woman who demands this togetherness. I've worked with couples in which the man, like Allen, enjoyed sports and action movies and expected his wife to watch television with him. Going out on her own was viewed as rejecting him. "She should spend time with me," he complains, not quite willing to accept that football bores her and viewing one more car chase on television might be the last straw. Another man resented his wife's commitment to her creative writing classes. He wanted her to spend her evenings on the couch with him and their sons, instead of writing in her journal or working on her short stories. He thought she was shutting him out, and she thought he was being selfish. This couple eventually found one activity—besides their children—they could enjoy doing together. That took some of the pressure off, but they still argue constantly.

Sometimes a partner's need for solitude can be threatening, but as one client of mine said, "I wish he understood that my need to be alone to read and meditate is not a need to be away from him. It's a need to go to myself, to be with my own thoughts." If people could understand this one simple concept, there would be a lot less conflict surrounding time spent together.

My best advice is to avoid looking at other people's marriages as the model for your own. Create your own agreements and ground rules. When you hear yourself saying, "My mother always watched television with my father....", or "My father always talked to my mother about....", stop and listen to yourself. Are you getting your expectations from your parents' marriage? When some people examine this, they find they really don't want that model anyway. Do your own thing; nowadays you have this freedom if you choose to take advantage of it.

A Date With Your Lover

Another myth that survives despite all evidence to the contrary: Sex should always be spontaneous—planned sex is not romantic. Is that so?

Andrea made all the arrangements for her date with her lover. She packed a sexy nightgown, arranged for the baby sitter, made the reservation at the luxury hotel, and ordered wine to be delivered to the room. The month before, Ed had made the arrangements and told her where to meet him. Yes, this was a monthly rendezvous, one that Andrea and Ed had been regularly arranging for five years. They'd have a wonderful dinner and then retreat to their hotel room for a night of sex and intimacy. Before they settled on this sexy date idea, they'd had little time for romance or intimate moments. Two jobs, three kids, a big house, community commitments, and two ill parents had all but insured that sex was infrequent. They also began to feel distant from one another and uncomfortable with the quick sex they managed now and then.

I've heard other couples talk about making dates for sex, and it often works out very well. Andrea and Ed said that they became far more tolerant of all the hassles and demands once they knew they had this one night just for themselves. Sometimes the talking was as important as the sex, particularly because they had family and career concerns, which they had little time to discuss at home. They had sex at other times as well; their once-a-month tryst wasn't the only time they got together. However, both agreed that their relationship was better in all ways because of this one special night.

You Go Your Way, I'll Go Mine

Mike and Rhonda came to counseling because they couldn't solve another kind of problem, this one also based on a common myth. Mike put it well: "Once you start taking separate vacations, you might as well get divorced." Nosy neighbors and meddling families are probably responsible for perpetuating this myth. I've heard people gossip for weeks because Susie and Jim went away for a week—to two separate destinations! Tut, tut, something must be wrong with that marriage.

More than most couples I see, Mike and Rhonda had much in common. They even worked together and had created a successful consulting business—so successful they could certainly afford to indulge their different tastes in travel. Yet even the thought of this shocked Mike. He was sure it would lead to the demise of their marriage. Rhonda thought it would be great. She would fly to Greece and spend ten days island hopping and looking at ancient ruins. Next year, she'd go off to Argentina and Chile. And next year...

Mike was really upset now. All he really wanted was a beach and a golf course. He had hoped that Rhonda would find something to enjoy at the same location. But he had to admit that he didn't want to go to Greece and wasn't thrilled about Argentina as a destination either. Mike was a mature man, and when he realized that Rhonda genuinely didn't care to be in the great outdoors, he agreed to give the separate vacations idea a one-year try. As it turned out, both liked the arrangement and have continued it.

Other couples have tried it and didn't like it. In those cases, they ended up compromising in order to be together. One couple worked out an arrangement in which he could go hiking in the mountains for two weeks with an adventure travel group and she could go to a nearby retreat to study yoga and enjoy some time alone. When they met up on the weekend after their first week apart, they were both relaxed and happy. This is now a regularly scheduled vacation break. Another couple worked out a similar arrangement involving weekend trips. He went fishing and she went on bicycle trips. They met back at a motel on Sunday evening.

The so-called right thing would be wrong for all the couples mentioned above. Imagine the futility of trying to fit all these individual interests into one vacation where every minute is "supposed" to be spent together.

Your Bed or Mine?

The other "separate" myth applies to bedrooms. As if it's any of their business, some friends and family members will assume that a marriage is just about over if the couple has separate rooms. (Have you noticed that when a new President and First Lady move into the White House, the whole country is informed about their sleeping arrangements, as if we can draw conclusions about their marriage based on this one fact?) In many situations, having two bedrooms is a beneficial arrangement. One of my clients chose separate rooms because she liked to read late at night and her husband needed to go to bed early in order to get up at 5:30 A.M. They were a sexy couple, not the roommates many people assumed, and each had a double bed to accommodate their romantic visits.

Some people are afraid to go with their own preferences for fear of gossip and assumptions on the part of others. But those who do follow what's best for them usually end up indifferent to what others think.

Compromise and More Compromise

Everyone knows that marriage is a fifty-fifty arrangement and the only way to success is through compromise. Well, maybe so, but sometimes the compromises may not be very conventional. Take Oscar and Georgene. She didn't like his sports-filled weekends and wanted him to watch the games only two weekends a month. I suggested that if Oscar agreed to this arrangement it might be with a grudging heart. Besides, he'd miss his routine. Instead, I thought Oscar should be allowed to watch his football in peace, and Georgene should come up with something she wanted from him that was unrelated to this weekend time. She chose to take an exercise class two nights a week and on Saturday morning. He would be responsible for their young children's dinner and bedtime rituals as well as Saturday morning breakfast. Oscar thought this was fine and Georgene went off happily by herself several times a week.

Hold the Ketchup

Lenore and Mitch are my ketchup lovers. They fought over which brand they preferred. Lenore, a penny pincher, didn't want to buy his brand because it cost too much. Mitch didn't like her brand because it was too watery. Meanwhile, Mitch was resentful because Lenore wouldn't buy his favorite kind of ketchup, but putting him in charge of shopping triggered her resentment about money. Can you believe this? Yes, it sounds trivial. So what was the real problem?

Like many such trivial arguments, the issue was actually about control, specifically about Mitch's control over many things in their lives. Mitch didn't understand this and needed an example.

Without having to think for a second, Lenore gave him one. Mitch kept his tools in a spot in the basement that Lenore had wanted for her sewing space. Mitch's attitude had been that she should simply make other plans—the space was his. Naturally, she resented the cavalier way he had divided up their jointly owned basement.

The problem here wasn't really compromise. Rather, it was Mitch's need to understand that his independent decisions, made without regard for Lenore's feelings, had eaten little holes in their relationship. While she never openly stated her resentment, she retaliated by refusing to buy the ketchup he liked. They worked on deepening their understanding of each other and one day, Mitch just moved his tools out of the space Lenore wanted. Lenore went out and bought the ketchup. It's become a family joke.

I believe that the fifty-fifty principle is better applied to likes and dislikes, rather than an absolutely equal division of this and that. For example, perhaps one partner really likes to cook but hates to do yard work. Obviously, the time spent on each chore wouldn't be equal—after all, cooking has to be done every day. But one person might not mind, because he or she really detests mowing the lawn.

If you feel resentful about something that is going on in your marriage, examine it carefully and see if you are upset over the actual unfairness involved, or if control or perceived selfishness is the issue. When you can communicate about the other issue, you may be able to solve the little niggling things that cause so much tension. What if Lenore had said, "I won't buy your expensive ketchup because you're always telling me what to do, not because of the extra cost." This provides a direct line to the problem. Think of all the small arguments that could be avoided if we get to the heart of the matter.

Much miscommunication results when couples refuse to look behind the petty words that are thrown around casually. Some of this miscommunication may have to do with the differences in the ways men and women communicate, but it also may involve an unwillingness to look at another point of view.

Compromise is necessary, but it can be approached more creatively than most of us realize. Before you start making compromises, examine the situation and see if another underlying issue exists. Maybe you will find that the issue really is about green or brown carpeting or vacations at the beach. But, you may find that the so-called right compromise, one that seems obvious at first, may be wrong for you.

Second Chance

I know that statistically, second marriages are at least as likely to end in divorce as first marriages. However, I have seen some twice-married couples who seem to have moved past the control and perfection issues that seem to consume first-time husbands and wives. A man once told me that in his first marriage, the toothpaste tube issue was a big one. You know, the old squeeze from the bottom, or go with the middle dilemma that is the subject of jokes. "We just buy two tubes of toothpaste," he said. More than once I've heard second wives laugh off the problem of football on weekends, saying, "who cares, let him be." I've heard second husbands praise the careers of their second wife when they had been threatened by their first partner's success. It has occurred to me that it's too bad that the ability to adjust and compromise couldn't have been learned before the hard lesson of a divorce was necessary. And it's too bad some people never learn and carry their mistakes into the second marriage.

Keeping Secrets

Tiffany had once had an affair with Ralph. Now, a year after her marriage to Josh, she discovers that he and Ralph are friends. The men had known each other years before and had recently renewed their friendship. Ralph never said a word about the affair, but he and Tiffany openly acknowledged that they had once known each other. Josh didn't think anything about it.

But Tiffany couldn't leave well enough alone. For some reason, she felt guilty about this affair, although she and Josh had both had many relationships before they were married. So one evening, Tiffany told Josh about her fling with Ralph, and now she regrets it. It seems that Josh did not take this news gracefully. He was unable to maintain his friendship with Ralph and was angry with Tiffany, too. They've worked it out, but it did have negative consequences that might have been avoided if Tiffany had simply kept her mouth shut.

I usually recommend considering all the ramifications of "confessing" a secret, especially if you are doing it to relieve guilt. Of course some people will tell you that a good marriage is one in which there are no secrets. Close couples share everything; they hold nothing back. Everything can be forgiven, so let it all out.

Not so fast. In many cases, telling a secret hurts someone, so you must weigh the consequences. Will you be asking another person to keep the same secret? Who is being helped by revealing the secret? What are the possible ways for the other person to react?

Most people have private thoughts, sometimes thoughts they aren't proud of. Are they doing another person a favor by "confessing" them? If I tell you that I was once so angry with you that I plotted your murder in my mind, whom am I helping?

Most couples have found that they don't need to know every little ugly incident that occurred in a previous relationship or marriage. Most lovers and spouses don't need or want to know about the day you went to bed with two different men while you were engaged to good ol' Joe. They most certainly have no interest in the women who became wildly orgasmic the minute you entered the room. (You'd be surprised at the lack of discretion some people have.)

Spontaneity and intimate sharing enliven and enrich our relationships. But there are times when tact, discretion, and thoughtfulness should come first. If you must talk about something that could hurt your partner, find another confidant and churn it over with him or her first. This may go against contemporary conventional thinking, but it may turn out right in the long run.

Separate, But Still In Love

I'm fascinated by all the ways love relationships can be arranged. Take Bill and Carol, two independent film producers and script writers who have been together for fifteen years. No, they aren't married, although they have a formal commitment to each other that they negotiated and wrote. And much to the amazement of their families, they don't live together, at least not all the time. For about two years, Bill and Carol shared a large apartment, but they decided that because of the demands of their work and their often conflicting work habits and hours, they were better off with separate places. Now they are apart for two or three days and together at one another's place for a few days. They schedule their time together and arrange for individual private time, even when they are in each other's homes.

Few people can understand this couple's arrangement. Carol's brother thinks Bill should marry her. He assumes Carol wants this, but she doesn't. She likes things just the way they are. Bill has a grown child from a first marriage. Carol accompanies Bill to his family's weddings, graduations, and holidays. Bill, in turn, goes to Carol's family functions. Like people who actually live together, they discuss their plans, check their calendars, and are as devoted as any couple I've ever known.

Bill's mother used to say, "But what if one of them gets sick?" Three years ago, Carol had a bout with breast cancer and Bill couldn't have been more devoted. (Some of Carol's friends thought he'd run, but Carol knew better.) Bill was with Carol during her hospital stay, took care of her when she came home, and helped her through the trauma of chemotherapy. Bill's mother was finally convinced that this nonmarriage was as committed a relationship as many formal marriages.

There are many people who need privacy and freedom to pursue their work. Like actors who must be away for weeks at a time, or like artists and writers who must work alone, some people need privacy and solitude. When I asked Bill and Carol the ultimate reason for their separate living arrangements, it was their need to immerse themselves in their work. They have bucked the opinions of others for a long time in order to do what was right for them.

Similarly, long-distance romances are not automatically doomed, although few stay long distance forever. I've heard about couples who are quite happy seeing each other on weekends or for one long weekend every month. Unfortunately, I've also seen situations in which the two people never even tried to build the relationship because they assumed that long-distance romances are doomed.

Irene and Tyrone live in separate studio apartments in the same building, and people keep asking them when they are getting married, when they are moving in together, and what's going on here anyway? Irene and Tyrone are in their fifties, and neither cares to marry, thank you. They like coming and going as they please. While not as emotionally close as Bill and Carol, this couple has worked out the level of intimacy they want in their lives. I've counseled people for whom this kind of relationship was particularly satisfying when they each had children to raise or other family demands to cope with. The other's home was a safe haven, a place that didn't have all the difficulties inherent in step-family situations. Love and devotion aren't lacking, but they have chosen an unconventional lifestyle.

LOVE CAN'T CONQUER ALL

No theme is more overworked in modern culture than romantic love. "Just you and me, kid, we'll fight the world, nothing can touch us." I've seen people put themselves into great jeopardy because they are convinced love will conquer all the problems.

Bruised and battered women who can't stop loving the man who hurt them are an extreme example of this attitude. What's more astonishing is the number of professionals who will actually encourage these women to fight violence by giving more love. I've seen situations in which doctors, counselors, and members of the clergy have been enlisted by family members to help convince a woman not to "break up the family." Loving a person who continually hurts you is not healthy; yes, it may be love, but it's sick love.

If you find yourself in a situation where you are sticking with a gambler, a drug addict, an alcoholic, or a verbally and emotionally abusive person, take a step back and try to see what's really going on. Seek out the help of a professional who is objective and does not have preconceived ideas about what *should* happen to a marriage. Some mental health professionals believe that marriages should be saved at all costs. This is the "right" outcome. When I was a new counselor I believed this too. But years of experience have taught me that separation and subsequent divorce is the best solution in many situations, especially those in which abuse or addictive problems are involved.

Again, there's no one right way, but if you are being pressured either to leave or to stay, step back and give yourself some time to evaluate your situation. Barbara was told that her husband's extreme jealousy was a sign of love. Her sister told her that most women would give anything for a man that possessive. But Barbara was a prisoner in her marriage. She wasn't "allowed" to go to the grocery store by herself, let alone have a job. Was this love? Barbara would sneak out of the house to see me, and finally, when for the fifth time her husband refused to go to counseling, she left. Barbara literally had to run to another state to get away from this dangerous man. Her sister still thinks she threw away a great guy.

Lance was pressured to leave his wife, a woman who suffered from serious depression. He was told that he was too young to sacrifice his life, too old to waste the rest of it on a sick woman, too handsome to settle for an empty marriage, and on and on.

The other part of the chorus encouraged him stick with her no matter what—God, duty, and love demanded it.

Lance stopped listening to others and began to listen to his own heart. After two more unsuccessful attempts to find the right treatment, his wife's physicians tried a new medication that eventually stabilized her illness. After several months, they were able to begin living normally again. Their counseling involved adjusting to living without the illness—they had forgotten how good it could be.

One day, Lance told me that although he loved his wife, a year before her breakthrough he had put a time limit on the marriage. If she was not better within two years, he'd reevaluate and feel free to make arrangements for her care and leave the marriage. "I faced the fact that I couldn't love her into health, but I wanted to give it more time."

The solution that Lance had come up with would have satisfied none of the people who harped at him about what he should do. However, he was listening to his own head and heart. He'd come up with a temporary solution that involved staying, but he gave himself permission to reevaluate. Happily, he was not pushed into this reevaluation and Lance and his wife settled into a peaceful relationship. Both are realistic and know the depression could strike again, but they are determined to fight it if that happens.

IT'S OKAY TO QUIT

You've tried counseling, you've tried being roommates, you've tried coaxing your partner into treatment for an addictive illness, you've tried threats, and you've tried a trial separation. Now you're tired. Sometimes all this work just won't work. As one client said, "Too much destructive behavior killed the love I once had. It died and won't come back." All the good advice from authority figures would not revive the love this woman once had for her husband of nineteen years. She ignored the angry, pleading voices and left her marriage.

I saw this woman to help her through a painful divorce, and working with another counselor, I helped mediate the settlement. I was genuinely happy for my client when the divorce was final. She pulled herself together and has created a wonderful new life.

You have a right to decide whether to get married, separated, divorced, or remarried. You can decide never to marry at all. You can put love aside and marry for convenience or money. If you decide to marry, you can arrange your relationship your way— separate bedrooms, separate vacations, sexy date nights, or as little contact as possible.

You've seen the many ways that real people have worked out their marriages, and even their divorces. Perhaps you're in the midst of a situation that needs a decision. If the examples in this chapter have expanded your thinking and opened your eyes to new options, then you are on your way to making decisions in your own way and in your own time. In intimate relationships, as in other areas of life, follow your own star. You'll be happier for it.

Five

Sex, Lies, and Affairs

Melanie is a bright, attractive, and ambitious woman in her mid-thirties, who is also raising a child by herself. Some years before she came to see me, her husband had said, "I need to explore new things in life. Marriage is beginning to feel like a trap." Two weeks later, he was gone, and Melanie started over. From the beginning of our work together, she had made it clear that she wasn't interested in remarrying any time in the near future. There were many reasons for this, not the least of which was her need to advance in her career in order to make enough money to raise her child. She was a devoted single mother who didn't care to put much of her energy into even finding a man to date on a regular basis.

Yet Melanie's parents and friends were applying subtle pressure, such as offering to fix her up with the cousin of the neighbor down the block. They also were sending clear verbal messages: Go out and find a new man, your child needs a stepfather, you can't make it alone, you're missing out on life, and many more absolutes. For the most part, Melanie laughed off this pressure and went her own way. Melanie did, however, greatly miss a regular sex life.

During one of our sessions, Melanie told me that she'd gone away on a weekend business trip, and after working hours, she'd spent about ninety percent of her time in bed with a single coworker. She'd had a great time and came home relaxed and invigorated. I asked her if she now expected to be dating this man whose company she'd obviously enjoyed so much. "Oh no," she said. "He has a girlfriend. I was in the mood for sex and he was available and interested, and, as it turned out, good in bed. That's all there was to it—it was a fun fling. And it was safe sex too." Melanie never expressed a moment's regret over her actions, even when some people in her office started gossiping about her being "had" by this man. She just laughed and said, "I wasn't had—I had him."

In cases like Melanie's, the voices of convention and authority immediately start to buzz around in everyone's head. Some common reactions might be:

- Sex for sex's sake is wrong.
- Casual sex is always wrong, dangerous, stupid, leads to low self-esteem, and so on.
- Melanie should have thought about the man's girlfriend. She was participating in his "cheating" behavior.
- Melanie is a selfish woman in the first place because she isn't interested in a serious relationship.
- Workplace sex always leads to disaster. Melanie should have chosen someone outside her office.
- Extramarital sex is a sin under any circumstances.

We probably could add some other adages based on conventional wisdom and religion. There are people who believe that sex outside of marriage is always immoral, and these people probably would not make Melanie's choice. And if they did stray from their religious precepts, they most likely would feel guilty. Certainly they would not have had the relaxed—even contented—attitude Melanie had. A therapist might work with such a client to explore any feelings of guilt and the reasons he or she acted in a way that was contrary to stated beliefs. None of this applied to Melanie. Although she was a thoughtful, ethical person, she did not have deeply held rigid rules about sexual behavior.

Melanie's sex-for-sex's-sake weekend affair was never a particularly important issue in our therapy sessions, although I was prepared to talk about it if she was concerned about any aspect of the fling. But, she believed that she had a right to sexual pleasure, and she also maintained that she'd chosen the man well. While he was dating another woman, he wasn't married. He was a decent, fun-loving sort of man, someone she trusted, but in whom she had no long-term interest.

What about the consequences? For some people, the fact that Melanie brought sex into the workplace, so to speak, was one big mistake, another "wrong" sure to provide material for the office gossips. I wondered whether this would bother her, or if she would be punished in some subtle way at the office. After all, she violated the unspoken rule about not becoming involved with a coworker.

When I asked her about this, she said that she wasn't bothered by others' opinions in this matter. She also believed that having a fling with a peer was not viewed the same way as being involved with the boss might have been. As an afterthought, she added, "I guess I would have spent the night with the boss instead if he had been the appealing one. There's always another job to be had." The point is, of course, that Melanie had made decisions based on her values and was willing to take the consequences for her actions.

In some cases, a client might have brought this information to the therapist in order to examine the motivation for having a casual fling. I've known women who do experience some loss of self-esteem if they violate sexual standards they have established for themselves; sometimes these standards are ones they haven't examined closely. They may believe they are flawed women because they are divorced or not interested in having a deep, serious relationship with a man. Some women would like to have a sex-for-sex's-sake affair, but they fear the consequences, mostly their own self-judgment and that of others. In fact, some people spend endless hours in therapy analyzing what took Melanie about fifteen minutes to decide on her weekend trip—that sex for sex's sake was a great option for her at that point in her life. She was so confident about it, that I doubt anyone could have convinced her she'd done something wrong or dumb.

SEX—NOBODY'S OR EVERYBODY'S BUSINESS?

There is probably no other area of human life—except possibly raising children—that prompts people to have strident views. This is wrong, that is right. This is right only if... What's more, many people don't restrict their strident views to their own sexual behavior: they believe they know what is best for everyone else as well.

Because sexual consequences can be complex and severe, it makes sense to consider one's behavior carefully. It also makes sense for society to be involved in the shaping of sexual mores and attitudes. I don't advocate for a minute that we all adopt an "everything and anything goes" attitude. Sexual behavior involving children, to give an obvious example, is everyone's business. However, I also believe that most sexual behavior between consenting adults falls into the category of nobody else's business.

Sex and the whole arena of love relationships are areas where professionals and lay people alike impose—consciously or unconsciously—their standards on other people. Melanie's family and friends couldn't understand her lack of interest in having her own man. What about her child? What about her financial stability and her future? With such conservative views, you can imagine what these people would have thought of her weekend fling. However, Melanie kept her own counsel and simply never told anyone, except a close friend and me, her therapist, about the event. Although she was not ashamed of her views, she wisely chose to discuss them only with those she trusted.

Noelle, another young single parent, had chosen a path entirely opposite Melanie's. She simply wasn't interested in any kind of casual sexual encounter and preferred to wait for a man with whom she could be emotionally involved. Because she was not actively looking for a new man, preferring to concentrate on her career and motherhood, she hadn't yet found anyone special. The thought of sex with a relative stranger was a turnoff rather than a turn-on. Sex for the sake of sex was simply not in her best interests at that time. As she put it, "Going without sex for a year or two may be unpleasant, but I won't die from it."

Interestingly enough, Noelle's decision, though entirely different from Melanie's choice, was also subject to criticism. Several of Noelle's friends believed she was foolish to "save herself" until the right man came along. They accused her of being old-fashioned and out of step with the times. "It's been over a year," one friend said, "and you haven't had any sex. You should find someone, *anyone*, and have a fling—someone sexy and gorgeous. But of course, practice safe sex." Fortunately, Noelle could let all this good advice roll off her back, and she made her own choice.

Conventional wisdom tells us that sexual mores are based on a set of standards that should last a lifetime. Therefore, these standards should be laid out early in life and we should stick to them. That sounds good, but I've seen too many cases where this kind of rigidity deprived some people of pleasure and forced others to live out someone else's idea of a healthy sexual life.

Melanie and Noelle, on the other hand, each looked into her own heart and came up with perfectly good outlooks based on individual attitudes, beliefs, opinions, and evaluations at the time. It's entirely possible that they could each change; next year they might reverse their positions because their needs and circumstances are different.

SEXUAL REVOLUTION OR EVOLUTION?

Once upon a time there was a firm set of rules about sexuality. Good girls shouldn't do it before marriage; good boys shouldn't do it either, but we'll look the other way; women don't enjoy sex as much as men do; no one should have extramarital affairs, but men can have one or two and all is forgiven. And finally, there is the belief that sex is by nature somewhat sinful, but marriage makes it okay—just don't make too much of it.

There are no doubt variations on this general theme, but I think you get the idea. At one time, most people agreed on the basic set of rules, even if they didn't follow them all the time—and indeed they didn't. About thirty years ago, however, voices both strident and soft started challenging the conventional rules, and women began to shout, "Foul, double standard, no fair, we demand different rules for this game." Things did change, and while we obviously don't have an entirely new set of sexual mores that everyone can agree on, almost everything is up for consideration and discussion.

The sexual revolution has now become more of an evolution. Women like Noelle and Melanie are making choices based on their own needs at any given time, rather than being guided by the old morality, which didn't really offer them a choice. They are sometimes making choices that seem contrary to the new sexual freedom and believe those choices are just fine too. Of course, single women were having sex long before 1960, but they weren't supposed to, so they didn't automatically consider that they had a wide range of options.

Nowadays, the openness about women and sex has radically changed attitudes and, most important, behavior. Few people still hold on to the notion that women are only sexual when they're married or that they don't enjoy sex much anyway—no religious principles have been strong enough to keep that myth alive. And I wonder just how many people believed it anyway, headache jokes notwithstanding. It served a purpose, albeit a negative one, but now that purpose is gone.

Speaking of headaches, that worn-out joke has a new life. Today, men are getting the headaches as they strive to live up to the expectations they believe have been placed on them now that women demand to enjoy sex too.

Let's look at some of the sex myths that currently are confusing people.

A headache is a good excuse.

It's better to plead a headache than hurt your mate's feelings. Men in particular feel rejected when turned down for sex. Better to lie and keep them happy. The flip side to this: If the man doesn't think he can perform, it's better to plead a headache because this demanding sexual creature will never understand why he can't make love. Of course, it's best to tell the truth, but in some situations, a little subterfuge isn't so wrong.

Women should never say no to sex.

Please your man at all costs—that's what some women are told. Norma was too tired for sex every night, but Don insisted. Norma was taught that she shouldn't say no. Naturally, she became angry and hostile while performing her "duty." Even though there is plenty of support nowadays for the idea that Norma should express her true feelings, the old rule was so ingrained that she felt guilty when she said no to sex.

By the time this couple came to me for counseling, the anger and misunderstanding had been building for years and spilled over to many other areas in their marriage. Once again, the right thing is being truthful, and in this case, truth would have been better in the long run. But let's look at another example.

Women should never fake orgasms.

I really enjoyed working with Kay, a woman typical of our changing times. She and her husband, Jay, had been married for ten years and had two children. Kay had a great career and she and

Jay were happy in most ways. For most of her adult life, Kay had enjoyed sex—sometimes she even loved it. But during these hectic years of taking care of the children and being busy with work, she just wasn't in the mood as often as Jay was.

Jay was respectful about his wife's diminished desire for sex, although he was also disappointed by it. When the couple did have sex, Jay wanted it to be just right. He wanted to take all the time necessary for Kay to have an orgasm. But Kay didn't care that much about it. So, from time to time, in order not to hurt her husband's feelings, she faked it.

The chorus of condemnation sang loud in Kay's head—she thought she should feel guilty about faking an orgasm, no exceptions. But Kay didn't feel the guilt she thought she should feel. She just didn't think it was that big a deal. "When the pressures ease up," she said, "I'm sure that I'll want more sex again. Right now, I don't want to hurt Jay's feelings and I don't want to drive him away. I like the closeness of sex, but sometimes I'm too tired to make a big deal of it. This seems like a good compromise to me." It seemed so to me too.

I would never recommend that women fake orgasm all, or even most, of the time. It isn't fair to their partners or to themselves. However, I was hard pressed to find anything particularly wrong with Kay's solution. After all, what was wrong with sparing her husband's feelings? She was trying to keep the delicate balance between meeting the demands of her life and still having a pleasant relationship with her partner. As most people know, this isn't easy. Kay's solution seemed to work for her, despite the conventional wisdom of experts who would argue that she is wrong.

Most women—and men—will admit to faking an occasional orgasm. They probably thought nothing of it until they heard experts telling them that they were being dishonest and possibly even destructive in the relationship. That may be so if women routinely fake sexual pleasure. The experts rightly say that if women always fake, then their lovers don't have the opportunity to find out what they like in bed. And if the faking goes on for very long, the man will feel deceived.

I agree with these experts, and encourage women to talk to their sexual partners about their needs, what they like, and what brings them to orgasm. But this is a long way from a hard and fast rule which states "thou shall not ever fake." I hope women will put this one to rest where it belongs. Let's give ourselves credit for knowing in our own hearts when day-to-day sexual decisions make sense and when they are potentially harmful.

If you truly love your mate, you'll do anything.

Patty and Dick are not in counseling. I read about them in a book about open marriage. They insist they are happy with the sexual and social freedom they have agreed on, and I say, no matter how wrong it seems for anyone else, if the arrangement makes them happy, it's okay. Jackie, on the other hand, came to me for counseling because her open marriage was making her miserable. She had agreed to it because it was the only way her husband would continue the marriage. But, obviously, it was wrong for Jackie, and she spent all her time wondering what her husband was doing behind her back, supposedly with her consent. In this case, "anything" was too much for Jackie.

Sex should be spontaneous.

Many people think that scheduling sex is unnatural or even wrong. However, think about how exciting and romantic affairs generally are—precisely because sex is scheduled. The two people look forward to their time together all day or even all week. Married people can look forward to scheduled sex as well. Sometimes in this hectic life so many of us seem to lead, scheduled sex is the only way to have any sex at all.

Sex among the elderly is wrong.

You probably would be surprised to learn how many people actually frown on older people having sex, particularly if the people in question are their mothers and fathers. I once heard some grown-up children talking about their seventy-four-year-old mother's remarriage as being "just for companionship." How did they know that their mother wasn't finding great joy in a rejuvenated sex life? Some people view sex among the elderly population as something of a joke and even a bit "indecent." Yet recent studies have shown that elderly people are staying sexually active and enjoying it.

A sexless marriage won't work.

I've known of couples for whom sex was an extremely infrequent event—some couples never had sex. If both people agree to a sexless marriage, then why is it wrong? Conflict only enters the relationship if one or the other person in the marriage is dissatisfied with the arrangement.

"Kinky" sex is always wrong.

By kinky sex I mean group sex, spouse swapping, threesomes, and so on. However, some people even believe that such things as oral or manual sex or sex in a variety of positions and places falls into the category of kinky. I once counseled a woman who had been taught that sex was "proper" only at night and in a bed. For this woman, oral sex on the couch in the middle of the afternoon was kinky. And contrary to popular belief, many men are more inhibited than women. I've counseled men who were uncomfortable with their wives' desire for so-called kinky sex.

The point is, as long as the two people involved agree and no one gets hurt, any sexual practice is okay. Spouse swapping and threesomes are important to some people, and they claim these practices help keep their marriages alive. As long as everyone consents, who is to say that these people are mistaken, even though conventional wisdom holds that this behavior is wrong? However, no one has the right to demand that you participate in this multi-partner behavior. And I would always ask why this behavior is so attractive to your partner, man or woman. Pressured sex is never ethical.

SOMETIMES WRONG IS WRONG

When I first began to notice the wide range of sexual choices my clients made and were happy with, AIDS (acquired immune deficiency syndrome) had not yet arrived on the scene. There is no question that this fatal disease has changed the sexual behavior of many people. Melanie was quick to point out that she and her weekend lover practiced safe sex. She was aware of what she needed to do to protect herself. Apparently, so was her partner. In addition, during the 1980s, clients of mine have come to the conclusion that extramarital affairs can be dangerous and their once casual attitude about them has changed.

A reevaluation about who to have sex with, and under what circumstances, is entirely appropriate in these days when AIDS and other sexually transmitted diseases are rapidly spreading and affecting all segments of our population. I am also predicating this discussion of sexual rights and wrongs on the following principles:

- Sexual behavior that puts another person at risk is *always* wrong. "At risk" means having unprotected sex or knowingly exposing another person to a disease such as genital herpes, gonorrhea, or AIDS. Some sexually transmitted diseases aren't fatal, but that fact doesn't mean it's okay to take chances.
- It's not okay to risk unwanted pregnancy for the sake of spontaneity or any other excuse. Both men and women need to carefully avoid taking these chances.
- Sex by coercion, trickery, or force is always wrong. There are no exceptions here; rape is rape, threats are threats.
- The sexual choices we're talking about here involve consenting adults. Involving children in adult sexual behavior is always wrong—and this boundary never moves.

These points might seem obvious, but I don't want to proceed any further with the discussion of sexuality without making it clear that irresponsibility in sexual matters is not what we're talking about here. Nor am I advocating that people behave like Melanie, Noelle, or any of the clients whose stories follow. What I am saying, however, is that what might seem wrong by old rules or in the judgment of others, often works well for people facing the kinds of decisions we're about to explore.

Flirting, Flattery, and Other Games

It's wrong to play games—or so we're told. There are volumes and volumes of advice books about finding a relationship and keeping it going, and most experts in this field tell us that it's not nice to play games. We should always be honest and if love is true, games shouldn't be necessary anyway.

I'm not so sure.

When I was a young woman, I had been dating a man for three years—everybody thought we were as good as engaged. But somehow he just couldn't seem to make a commitment (yes, this happened back then too). I decided to force the issue by telling him I'd met someone else. Shortly after my announcement, my boyfriend asked me to marry him. Of course, I hadn't met anyone else. It was a little white lie, but it worked. We've been married for over thirty years. The wrong thing turned out to be right for me.

Would I advise other people to engage in this kind of game? Not necessarily, but I wouldn't say it's always wrong. I've had friends and clients who have been too honest, and are finally sick of it. Their lovers or mates seemed to take them for granted. So they sparked a little jealousy by making plans with other friends, or by not giving an hour-by-hour report of their day. Common sense can guide us here. A spirit of fun can help also. The idea isn't to hurt the other person, it's to add some excitement to the relationship. I don't recommend ever hurting someone deliberately, but we don't have to be taken for granted either.

In the game of love and relationships, we use what we have. If you can tell that the stranger across the room finds you appealing, don't fight it, use it. Worry about getting to know him or her later. Sometimes that first significant look is enough to spark interest. It's not wrong to flirt and attract; it's all part of the initial dance.

Come Close, Go Away

Unfortunately, the dance can get complicated—even after a relationship has been established. In the early stages, it is common for one person to pursue and the other to distance. Many clients have mentioned how annoying this pattern is, and they are at a loss over what to do about it.

Patti, a woman in her late twenties, was having this problem with a boyfriend she'd had for about six months. They would spend a great weekend together, followed by silence on his end. The next week, he'd say he was busy and could only go out on Saturday night. Yet, when Patti, an independent young woman who always believed in being honest, asked him about his distancing behavior, he denied it. Apparently, he was not conscious of the way in which he ran from the intensity entering their relationship.

Patti needed to come up with a solution that wouldn't compromise—too much—her own desire for intimacy and honesty, but would stop the distancing behavior. First, she simply stopped suggesting ways to spend more time together. She even turned her answering machine on one evening when she thought he'd be calling her, forcing him to leave her a perplexed "thought you'd be home" message. Wasn't she always home on Thursday night? She never mentioned, and he never asked, where she'd been, but over a period of a month or two, her own distancing behavior worked.

Again, this may seem like game playing. And there might be circumstances where Patti's decision to distance would have become harmful to the relationship. But, in this case, it was all part of the dance two people often do when establishing an intimate relationship. In this example, it was the man doing the distancing, but that isn't always so. Women can be just as afraid of commitment and intimacy as men. And, men may want to counteract it in the same way.

I'll Do Anything For You

Sometimes things that are potential problems turn out not to be actual problems under certain circumstances. Take manipulation and flattery, for example. Fran, a neighbor of mine, seems to be able to get her husband to do just about anything she wants. For example, she likes to visit her mother and she prefers that Abel go along even though he doesn't enjoy these visits, and he almost always goes. Abel gives up his prized baseball games on television to go with Fran because, I am sure, she tells him what a kind, caring person he is for coming with her. Sounds manipulative, doesn't it? But Abel actually is a kind, caring person.

No doubt some people would say that Fran has a problem. Why can't she leave the man alone? Why does she need his company on these visits? Why does she want to deprive him of his favorite relaxation? All of these questions are valid. I ask them, too. But, who am I to argue with success? Fran and Abel are a loving couple. My point here is that we can't necessarily see into other people's lives and say what is right or wrong. Manipulation and flattery are generally considered behaviors that are clearly wrong—except when they seem to work.

I've seen other situations where flattery and manipulation were used cruelly and with the intention of coercing another person in unreasonable ways. Conscience and genuine goodwill are important in all our relationships. If I heard Fran laugh at her husband or ridicule him for being susceptible to her flattery, I would no longer respect her choice.

It goes without saying that manipulation and false flattery are not okay when used to coax another person into a sexual relationship. I've known women and men who had a false sense of pride over their ability to accumulate [...] goodwill is absent, manipulation and flatte[ry are] more than trickery.

The Sexual Résumé

Not long ago, Eva, a woman in her late forti[es...] because she had been having difficulties getting past the first date with a number of men. She was attractive and accomplished; her personality seemed bright and pleasant, yet the men she encountered seemed to run away in short order. When we looked at this more closely, it became apparent that Eva was spilling her life history during the first dinner, often before the salad plate was taken away. "I believe in putting the cards on the table," she said. "I've been married twice, I've got five kids, and I've done a share of running around. The sooner they know all about me, the sooner they can make up their minds. Anyway, I don't like to keep secrets, and some of these men won't reveal a thing."

Eva hadn't always been so open. In fact, this quest for instant honesty was part of a new resolve. But how well was it serving her? I didn't tell Eva what to do, but I did tell her what I've learned over the years about the danger of revealing too much too soon. I have seen so many clients rush to reveal all their secrets, especially the deep, dark ones. They believe they are being deceitful if they don't admit to having had foolish affairs or one-night stands or any number of things. They even talk about all the problems they are having with their children or ex-spouses. All this on a first date? Please.

It's All in the Timing

It isn't being dishonest to refrain from revealing everything in one evening or even over several dates. All your past romances might never need to be discussed. Obviously, past marriages must be revealed, but not necessarily on the first date. Timing, as they say, is everything. When Kim and Martin came to see me for counseling, he was furious because she had never told ... about a brief marriage she'd had during college. They'd been ...arried for five years, and her mother let the secret "slip" during a holiday party.

Martin felt betrayed, and he wondered what other secrets were being withheld. When asked why she hadn't talked about the marriage, Kim said, "I wanted to, but not when we were just getting to know each other, and then after a while, it almost seemed too late. It was a timing problem."

Kim is right. Timing is crucial. But it isn't fair to be silent about important events in our lives, and a past marriage certainly fits into this category. How many children we have, our education, crucial facts about our families, what our job is, and so forth are important. Eventually, Martin began to understand that Kim's judgment might not have been great, but she never meant to keep the secret. It's just that as time passed, in her eyes, it became too late to share that detail from her earlier life. It didn't take long for Martin and Kim to patch things up, and they began getting along again.

Eva also had a timing problem: She was handing over an entire sexual résumé along with her life story. There are no doubt parts of our life story that must be told to a potential partner, but on the second, third, and fourth dates. The sexual résumé isn't anyone else's business, and besides, it removes any mystery a person has. Why not keep the other person wondering a bit?

Most of the time, we know what is wise and what is foolish in the areas of love and sex. But too often, we follow rules that we didn't make up in the first place. There are times when honesty is indeed the best, and only ethical, policy. But there are other times when discretion is our best course. That's why we should think carefully before we jump in with our stories. I believe that if you make your own judgments, based on what seems wise to you at the time, you won't ruffle too many feathers or rock too many boats—except perhaps those that need it.

It's My Affair—and It's None of Your Business

When I was a young therapist I believed strongly that extramarital affairs were wrong, and that was that. Most of my colleagues agreed, and while we did not necessarily make moral judgments—at least out loud—breaking off an illicit affair was considered a successful outcome in therapy. But I've learned over the years that my original ideas were based on a faulty premise: that affairs are always destructive to relationships. Well, some are, and some aren't.

Rita was forty when she came to see me, ready for the first time to really work on her own life. She was just about finished raising her children and she had made many accommodations in her marriage, which in numerous ways was a strong one. Rita loved Milton, but right from the beginning (on their honeymoon, in fact), he had shown almost no evidence of passion and was a rather inept lover on the rare occasions when he was interested in sex. Milton also had no interest in talking about the problem. This disappointed Rita greatly, but she gradually had accepted her situation and found satisfaction in other areas of her life. As many women do in their marriages, she had "settled"—sort of.

By the time Rita came to therapy she had been seeing a married man for two years. They were in love with each other, but they loved their spouses too. She wanted help in coping with this emotionally complex situation. The complexity was more of an issue for me than it was for Rita. My inclination would have been to help Rita end the affair, work on the marriage or get out of it, but not to help her get comfortable with the affair.

Yet as I got to know Rita, listened to her thoughts and feelings, I began to see that her decision to maintain the status quo was the right one for her. In her own mind, the affair was justified. She'd been sexually deprived for years, and her husband didn't seem interested in the romantic side of their marriage. They lived like loving friends, but she also saw no reason to either divorce him or tell him about the affair. The lover she'd taken was in the same situation in his marriage. As far as I could see, no one was directly being hurt.

About a year after her counseling ended, I spoke with Rita and she was still content with the situation. Her lover was happy with the arrangement, too. The extended period of secrecy still concerns me, but as Rita said, "It's my affair, I'll handle it."

I think we can learn a lot about ourselves by listening to our internal reactions to Rita's story. Some people would say:

- She should leave the marriage if she isn't sexually fulfilled.
- Her husband is bound to find out anyway.
- What about her lover's wife?
- Sex outside of marriage is always wrong—she's morally unfit.
- What about her children?
- It isn't healthy to live two lives.

Obviously all these statements have some validity. However, let's look at what was best for Rita. She had been successful in balancing the demands of two relationships. The fact is, and we all know it, people make compromises and accommodations. They consider their options, they look at the good and the not-so-good, and they adjust. Rita's way of adjusting gave her renewed energy to live her life in the marriage. She enjoyed her husband's company and didn't choose to leave. And, if all men and women who are not sexually fulfilled left their marriages, the divorce rate would climb even higher.

When we make our choices and live with them, there is always risk. Some people would rightly (for them) conclude that the best answer would be to leave the marriage and find someone else. Others would stay and end the affair, out of conscience or out of fear. And I concluded that there was no *one right answer*.

Rita chose what seemed to work best for her. Circumstances could change. One of the spouses could learn of the affair, for example, and then another decision point would present itself. Rita and all involved would have to sort through the issues and come up with another choice.

The Two-Affair Family

Matt and Joan were a good looking couple in their late thirties. They came to me for counseling because they were having major arguments over money. Joan believed that Matt was stingy with her; Matt believed that Joan had a spending problem—she loved to shop. Just because he had money, Matt thought, there was no reason for Joan to spend it so freely. I worked with this couple for a few weeks and then, as I usually do, I had them each come in alone for some individual sessions.

Matt came first. When I asked him why he wanted Joan to spend less money when it appeared that he had plenty to spare, I got an answer I didn't expect. "Well, I've been having an affair for several years," he said, "and I've spent a lot of money on this other woman. Of course, I can't explain this expense to Joan. We don't have as much money as she thinks." Things obviously were getting complicated. I suggested that perhaps he was being unfair to Joan and dishonest in his relationship with her.

"Not really," he said, "she's been seeing another man for years. But she doesn't know that I know about him. That's the way I want to keep it. But I don't want her to know about Jenny—it might upset her." So much for our session.

I was not finished hearing the unexpected. When Joan came in for her individual session, she was eager to tell me about both her and her husband's affair. "I've known about it for a long time," she said, "but I don't want him to know that I know. He wouldn't understand why it doesn't bother me, and of course, it's because I'm free to have an affair of my own."

Professional confidentiality prevented me from revealing these affairs, but I did try to encourage this couple to be more honest with each other. Honesty, I believed, would help them resolve the money issues and other problems, too. But neither was willing to talk about this. To this couple, the marriage issues were the only important ones; the affair issues were separate. In this case, the "secrets" that weren't really secrets hampered their progress and they terminated counseling shortly thereafter.

Because I work with so many couples, it's not surprising that I hear about partners' affairs. Nowadays, the double standard is all but gone, and many women feel quite justified about having affairs of their own. It's an issue many men must face in a new way.

Why people stay in marriages is a puzzle that no one has solved. But sometimes people seem to believe that the affair acts as a bandage that holds the marriage together, or stops the wounded relationship from becoming worse. Although I continue to believe that affairs are not good for most marriages and most people, it appears that many people are not willing to either leave marriages or work on the problems. For them, affairs help them to stay, rather than help them to leave.

Single people who wonder why their married lovers don't leave their marriages would do well to keep this information in mind. Matt's and Joan's lovers might wait a long time. It's possible that for this couple, the "secret" affairs combined with the tension over money might actually spark excitement in their relationship. Again, I'm not advocating this, and as a therapist, I thought the whole situation was headed for disaster. But, I could be wrong.

Affairs Don't Always Hurt People

In the best of all possible worlds, people would marry for love, get along well, be great lovers, and grow old having been faithful to the end. In the real world, as we all know, it doesn't always work this way. While it's difficult to say for sure just when an affair won't hurt another party, I have seen situations in which no one suffers. Rita and Milton, mentioned previously, could turn out to be a couple who can go through a lifetime without having to confront her infidelity. No one can predict these things absolutely, and I've seen situations where people truly can say, "No regrets."

Moira was deeply grieving when she first came to see me. Her married lover of seventeen years had died, and her grief was extremely difficult to handle because she couldn't talk about it with other people. No one in her family knew about her lover, and only a few friends were aware of Moira's long-term affair.

I had expected Moira to eventually express regret over giving seventeen years of her life to a man whose love she couldn't even acknowledge. However, after hearing Moira talk about the good and the bad of her affair, I believed that she meant it when she said, "I have no regrets. They were seventeen lovely years." Moira had started this affair when she was in her late forties and had already given up trying to find a man to marry. This man had filled many needs, and she was grateful for him. Recognizing that even her close friends would call this "wrong," she kept her affair secret, but she never believed it was wrong for her.

Part of therapy is breaking through defenses and what could be considered illusions. For example, Moira could have kept on looking and found a man to share a life with, rather than starting an affair with a married man. She could have learned to live happily as a single woman without a partner. We could have explored all these issues over a long period of time, but Moira dismissed those suggestions. She was sad that the man died, but she was happy she had the time with him while he was alive.

This was a clear case in which a therapist is challenged to examine his or her values. Even though conventional wisdom told me that she *should* have had regrets, it became clear that she didn't. Sometimes people know their minds well. Moira, bereft and lonely, needed someone to help her grieve, but certainly not someone who challenged her treasured seventeen years.

Norman Cares

Norman was much like Moira in that he had no intention of ending his affair and he had no regret about having entered into it. In some ways, his situation illustrates how a workable solution can be born from great tragedy. Norman had been married to

Laura for fifteen years, the first seven of which were quite romantic and happy. They were both musicians and each has the kind of sensitivity one finds in artists. When Laura was diagnosed with multiple sclerosis, their life did not change drastically at first. Until her physical deterioration made her unable to play the violin, life had continued to be rich and happy. But for the past three years, she had become increasingly bitter and angry and now spent most of her time in her room, sitting in a wheelchair. She needed help with every aspect of life, and Norman attended to most of her needs.

When Norman came to see me he was looking for help for Laura more than for himself. He had tried to coax her out of the house more; he had attempted to interest her in meeting new people. In fact, Norman had spent much of his time trying to help Laura cope with her illness and get as much enjoyment out of life as possible. In order to help himself, two years earlier he had begun an affair with Nora, who knew the situation and wasn't demanding that he leave Laura. "I'll love Laura forever," he said. "I won't leave her, but the affair helps me. Nora knows this; she has her own life and isn't asking for anything."

Was this so-called "wrong" choice hurting anyone? Not that I could see. Norman really didn't want to talk much about his affair. He was far more interested in helping his wife live her last years with some degree of happiness. I actually thought he was making the best of a tragedy. Nora, for reasons of her own, was content with the situation. It sounded like the best for all concerned. It doesn't happen often, but these situations do exist. Over the years I've learned not to judge before I know all the facts. Sometimes an affair really doesn't hurt anyone.

THE BEST REVENGE?

Remember Laurie and John? They were the couple in the first chapter who couldn't seem to start working on their marriage until Laurie had an affair to get even with John for having one first. As I said before, no therapist would ever advise taking such an action, but in this couple's case, it moved them forward. It was not the first time I'd seen sex used in various ways to get revenge.

There was May, who, on finding out that her husband was sleeping with a neighbor, went to visit her mother, leaving their two school-age children behind. She said she wouldn't return until Sidney agreed to marriage counseling and an immediate end to the affair. Sidney said yes, because he didn't want a divorce. He wasn't in love with the neighbor. To him, it was all just a mistake. May came home and Sidney expected a romantic reunion. After all, he'd said he was sorry, and he intended to make it up to May.

May, however, had a different plan. Until they were actually in marriage counseling, May refused to have sex with Sidney. She didn't talk about forgiveness or any possibility of a real reconciliation until she had a chance to think about what she wanted and talk about it in marriage counseling. Sidney had assumed that their marriage would resume as before. "I thought that when I said I was sorry," he explained in a bewildered voice, "that would be enough. The marriage counseling was just to appease her."

Sidney was in for a big surprise. It was two months before May was satisfied that his affair was truly just a casual, if badly considered, event. Furthermore, she used marriage counseling to begin making some demands on Sidney that she hadn't made before. For example, she was furious that Sidney wasn't sharing the housework, that "while he was off screwing our neighbor, I was doing all the cooking and cleaning. If he wants a marriage, then he'll have to start sharing more than our bed."

One never knows which nerve is going to be touched when an affair intrudes on a marriage. May could have walked away. She was that angry. But May had been angry before the affair. The issue of Sidney's unwillingness to do his part of the child care and housework had been festering for years. May, who worked full time, had felt cheated in this marriage anyway.

Sidney wanted the marriage, making it possible for May to

make the demands she had never been able to enforce before. In fact, Sidney ended up feeling more guilty about the years of pushing all the work off on his wife than he did about the affair.

I would not go so far as to say that May was happy about Sidney's affair, but she was certainly happy about the changes in her marriage that it had made possible. Wrong as the affair was, the results were positive. She was less angry, and Sidney was cooperating with her. It would, of course, have been better if May and Sidney had been able to equalize the work in their household without a hurtful affair as a catalyst. But this is real life. People don't always do what we'd like them to.

It is often too much to ask for a person to act noble and forgiving over sexual betrayal. Screaming, crying, and ugly accusations, although logical reactions, usually do not help the situation. Sometimes working out the issues helps, sometimes it's a question of licking one's wounds and trying to make the best of it. But sometimes, as we have seen, it can be revenge that ultimately works.

The Affair Can Mean the End

A word of caution: In the cases I've mentioned here, an affair didn't end the marriage. But many times it does. Again and again, I've seen sexual betrayal destroy, permanently destroy, a marriage. I've also seen both men and women so deeply hurt by affairs that even though they stay together, they are never able to rebuild a satisfactory relationship.

Alan and Selma worked hard in counseling. Selma had ended her affair with her boss and begged for forgiveness. The couple stayed together, but for as long as I knew them, Alan was never able again to enjoy sex with Selma—he simply could not erase the picture of his wife in bed with another man. Alan was clearly not a man who would even consider revenge, nor would I have ever suggested it.

George and Ella came to counseling hoping to revitalize their marriage after his affair was over. But instead of being able to reconcile, they became angry and ugly with each other as the major differences in their outlooks were revealed. In this case, the affair might actually have been for the best, because this couple really shared very little love. They had stayed in a marriage with little mutual satisfaction for too many years.

Sometimes, even though I try everything possible to help clients save their marriages, I view myself as a divorce counselor. There are those marriages where I find myself trying to help the clients separate in the most painless way possible. Interestingly enough, some couples come for marriage counseling because they want a divorce. If they go to counseling, they reason, they can say they tried, so this step helps relieve their guilt over really wanting a divorce all along.

Your Choice, Your Way

I hope that this chapter clarifies some issues in this complex sexual arena. All our lives we are put in positions where a sexual choice confronts us. Take time now to examine your own belief system about sexuality, fidelity, infidelity, and so on. Do you always know what is right? Are there gray areas in your own life—choices you made, opportunities you let pass by, because of some set of rules that were laid out for you to follow?

If you consult experts about sexual matters, listen carefully for their biases and values. Do they seem to have an agenda of their own? Are they open-minded and willing to consider that no one choice is right for everyone? In this, as in all other things, it is ultimately you who must decide and you who reaps the benefits or pays the consequences. Therefore, make sure your choices are your own.

Six

Parents, Siblings, and Children

John's problem was tearing him apart with guilt. He sat with his shoulders hunched over and stared at the floor during the entire hour of our first session together. "I suppose it's a simple problem, really," he said, "but I can't seem to solve it myself. It's my father. He's had a heart attack and needs help with his shopping and cooking and trips to the doctor. I've been doing these things, but I resent his demands and don't know if I can keep on doing this work."

John's situation wasn't unusual. Many middle-aged people find themselves helping out their parents, and it is often during these trying periods that old resentments emerge. The grown-up children find themselves angry and torn about helping their parents while still maintaining their own jobs and family life.

John's story, however, had a different twist. As our sessions continued, it came out that his father had been terribly cruel—although he had labeled it as simply being a "strict disciplinarian." In his household, discipline meant that John was severely beaten, from age two, for everything from talking too loud to not finishing his food to simply running around and being noisy, as children normally do. Even after many years of distance, John recalled the look of pleasure on his father's face as he inflicted his physical and verbal tortures. "I just can't get past the idea that he got perverse satisfaction and even pleasure from what he did," John said. "Now, whenever I look at him, helpless in his bed, it all comes back. But I feel guilty if I even think about walking out on him."

John's anger was made worse by the fact that his mother, being so terrified of her husband, had never stepped in to protect John. At age sixteen a life-changing event occurred. John finally struck back—he used his own superior strength to threaten his father and demand that the beatings stop. (Although this didn't happen in John's family, I've heard stories in which the father takes pride that the son has finally "become a man" and defends himself. This reversal of violent roles becomes a right of passage of sorts.)

In John's family, an uneasy peace was maintained until he left home on his seventeenth birthday. John joined the Navy and after his first few visits home were marked by hostility, he never returned.

Like many people in his situation, John appeared to have put the past behind him and eventually he'd married and had a family of his own. To his credit, he did not repeat the pattern of abuse, and in fact, had never hit either of his two children. He claims that keeping distance from his family made it possible to have a reasonably happy life. Sure, he has had the typical problems all marriages and families have, but he saw no reason to have contact with the people who'd hurt him.

Then without warning, a phone call from an aunt informed him of his mother's death a year before and of his father's recent heart attack. John felt forced to reenter the family arena. As an only child, it was up to him to decide what, if any, help he could or should offer to his father.

For many weeks, John and I sorted through his feelings about the events of the past and the scars they had left. He especially felt guilty because he didn't like or even love his ill father and had not experienced grief over his mother's death. "That just doesn't seem normal," he said.

If I've heard that once, I've heard it hundreds of times. And so, we get back to what normal means, particularly when it comes to relationships within families.

WHAT ARE WE TO DO WITH THESE FAMILIES ANYWAY?

Experts probably advise us about our family problems at least as much as they advise us about intimate relationships and sexual issues. Furthermore, at no time in our society's history has there been such dramatic change in family living and the structure of the family unit, not to mention what is considered acceptable behavior within a family setting. No wonder we have a difficult time defining normal.

At one time, we might have defined a family as parents and their children and the extended families they both bring to the marriage. Today, however, we have the so-called blended families created in second marriages. There are more single-parent households than ever before and we have gay and lesbian parents raising their children in same-sex couple homes. In our melting pot country, we have for a long time had intermarriage among different ethnic, racial, and religious groups.

Add to this marriage stew the changing role of women and we have many new challenges. While still not common, it is not unheard of for the father to become the primary caretaker of the children. In many households, women are demanding that their partners share equally in household work and child care. In fact, I've had women clients who left marriages because they were doing it all alone anyway. One woman said, "I was so resentful of my husband's unwillingness to share responsibilities that I finally decided that it was easier to just do it alone. At least I don't feel resentment toward him every minute of the day."

John's problem pointed up still another trend, that of calling abuse by its real name. For generations the same behavior that went on in John's home was prevalent in numerous families, but the adage, sometimes reinforced by religious teachings, to "respect your parents" was stronger than any reaction to the abuse. Some people of my generation, and those before me, even believed the myth that this kind of cruelty was "for our own good." Unfortunately, in cases where abuse was more subtle or the clients have rationalized it, psychiatric advice has not necessarily been helpful. However, in recent years, psychoanalyst Alice Miller and others have helped victims of childhood abuse step out of the closet and admit their pain—and often confront their parents. John, never thinking that he was part of a trend, had simply left home and tried to put it all behind him. Many people do just that, with varying results. In this area, we may not even be able to define what normal is.

Constant Urging To "Work It Out"

The overwhelming preponderance of advice still leans toward the idea that it is best if we can work out problems with our parents, children, and siblings. I find that in my own practice I still encourage people to try to reconcile, or at least maintain, as much contact as possible. However, no longer do I believe that it is the best solution in every case. I think, and so do many of my colleagues, that today people have many more options to choose from and they should be encouraged to explore all those choices before committing to maintaining family ties. Besides, "working it out" means something different from person to person. And in seeking advice, I wouldn't let any professional, religious advisor, or family member insist that he or she knows what is normal and right.

For John, the solution to the problem was a combination of things. First, he admitted that he didn't like or even love his father or his dead mother—what a relief it was for him to just say it, without qualifiers. The biological act of conceiving and giving birth does not automatically demand deference and love. Then, he gave himself credit for his part in creating a healthier, more peaceful home for his own family. Finally, he decided to draw lines in his own caretaking activities for his father. While choosing not to abandon him altogether, we worked to set limits.

I suggested that John call the local Council on Aging. What services were available to his father that would ease John's load? Within a few weeks, we learned that a senior citizen's van could take John's father back and forth to the doctor and the grocery store. A homemaking service could clean his house and prepare meals—and teach him how to take care of himself to the extent he could. At first, this man was angry; he had always had his wife to boss around and to wait on him. Now he was sick but not completely disabled and he, for the first time, had to take some responsibility for himself. What a shock. In a more loving relationship, John might not have had the heart to persist in making these demands on his father. But, given the family history, it wasn't that difficult.

Contrary to the popular myth of happy endings, reconciliations, and tearful confessions followed by forgiveness, John's father remained hostile and angry. He never "got it" that his earlier cruelty had driven his son away, although John did say as much to him. For his part, John came to a deep acceptance that yes, he had been cheated out of love from his parents, and having faced that, he was able to continue his own life free from guilt. Frankly, forgiveness never became an issue, because he felt so little for them in first place. I know that many people, professionals included, would believe that no one with John's background could live such a healthy, normal life. I disagree. There are many people like John in this world.

I've Sinned, So Say You're Sorry

Kitty still remembers the terror of being locked in a closet when she disobeyed a rule, and the beatings and verbal abuse will never be wiped from her memory. Like John, she'd had no recourse when she was a child, but unlike him, she had good memories of her childhood too. "It was like living in two different households—one of laughter and fun and the other of hatred and abuse," she said during an early session.

At her husband's urging, Kitty had sought counseling to help her reconcile with her parents. Her family doctor believed that her anxiety attacks would stop if she resolved the family issues. She genuinely wanted to continue a relationship with both parents. However, she also wanted answers and explanations, and during the past few visits to her parents, she had tried to get her father to tell her why he had been so cruel. She also had confronted her mother about her inability to protect the children from the explosive behavior.

Kitty's last visit to her parents had turned into an ugly scene, a long and drawn out shouting match. Kitty had decided not to subject her husband and children to the atmosphere in her parents' home again. After several months, however, she missed her mother and father and wanted to try again. She called her father and told him that she wanted to visit and would agree to avoid bringing up the past.

"Good," her father said, "and now you can say you're sorry for all the stories you made up and the heartache you've caused your mother. I want you to tell your brother that it was all in your imagination."

Kitty was shocked and horrified at the way her attempt to have an ongoing relationship with her father had backfired. She tried again and even wrote letters urging him not to make this demand because it was so dishonest. But he stood firm: no apology, no relationship.

Although Kitty didn't know it then, her father's reaction was typical of abusers, especially those who aren't abusive all the time. Out of hidden guilt, they try to deny the severity of their behavior and scapegoat someone else, in this case, the daughter. Kitty was becoming increasingly anxious as she accepted the fact that the only way she would find peace was to give in to her father's demand. (Actually, that's usually a false hope, anyway.)

Kitty's brother, Patrick, who also was abused, and her mother, wanted her to agree to her father's terms for a relationship. However, Kitty's husband was outraged at such a thought. While Patrick knew that Kitty was right about the facts, he didn't think the past was worth arguing about. He simply had made a different choice, one that apparently worked for him.

For Kitty, there was no "working it out." She couldn't acquiesce to her father's demands, and although she is sad about the fact she can't see her mother either, she has her integrity intact. To those who say that Kitty should have sought peace at any price, I say they don't have the right to direct other people's solutions. Kitty's gut feelings told her that she would never find peace if she had to live a lie.

Within the Extremes There Is Often a Middle Ground

Kitty's and John's stories are extreme, although frankly, what I hear from clients leads me to believe that their situations aren't rare by any means. However, in the absence of such extreme abuse or unpleasantness, most people are able to come to terms with parents, even those they don't like very much. Some situations are unpleasant, but not necessarily abusive.

An adult child may have to set limits with parents about such things as the way grandchildren are treated (either over-indulged or subjected to behaviors that could be harmful.) I once had a client who had to confront her mother-in-law about her petty shoplifting when she had taken her grandchildren to a mall. Naturally, these young kids were shocked when they witnessed their grandmother stealing. This situation did not result in a serious split, because it was brought up and resolved. Grandma agreed she was terribly wrong and agreed to go back to a therapist she had worked with years before. She understood that this was a serious issue.

A friend of mine had to limit contact with his mother because the woman was a compulsive critic. She was generous and even kind in other ways, but she couldn't stop making negative comments about his clothes (too casual), his haircut (too short), his job (not well-paying enough), the service in the restaurant (too slow), the doorman in his building (didn't recognize her after one visit), and on and on. So he gradually just came to accept that his mother was negative, that this wasn't going to change, and that he could limit his time with her as he chose. Once when she came for a weekend visit, the first thing she said at the airport was, "Your shoes need new heels." He stopped in his tracks and told her that if she was going to spend their visit picking him apart, he'd put her back on the next plane. Now this didn't solve the problem, but it took the edge off. Let's just say that it slowed her down a bit.

Fortunately, most problems grown children have with parents are workable. That's all good and most people do manage to maintain a relationship, even a close, loving one. But when the relationships aren't workable, when demands are too great, or the painful past too conflicted, then I recommend throwing out the advice books and following your inner truth. It may take time to determine what that truth is, but it's worth the effort.

SIBLING RIVALRY, OR, WHY WASN'T I AN ONLY CHILD?

Over the years, I've encountered numerous clients who haven't seen or spoken to their siblings in years. I've heard all kinds of reasons for the dislike, and some seem so insignificant that I must assume there are other, deeper reasons for the alienation.

If you have problems with a brother or sister, it may be necessary to look at the basic nature of sibling rivalry and how it occurs in the first place. It's been said that siblings almost always have some animosity because, with the birth of a second child, the first child will always feel displaced. From that time, competition for parents' attention and approval will almost always cause bad feelings.

In general, I encourage clients to renew lapsed relationships with their brothers and sisters because these bonds can enrich life and bring so much joy. Our siblings often share the same sense of humor and many of the same memories. They may even understand us better than other people possibly can. I usually tell clients that it doesn't matter if they weren't close to their brothers and sisters as children. As adults they have a chance to have a new, fresh relationship.

In my own case, I feel blessed to have such a warm, loving relationship with my sister, but as children we were not connected at all. We became friends later in life, after we both had established our lives away from family pressures. Certainly, my experience fits with the conventional wisdom that we should do everything possible to create a close family.

Although I have seen siblings renew ties the way my sister and I did, I have also seen cases when the wrong thing was indeed right for those involved, proving once again that conventional wisdom may be unworkable, or even stupid, in some cases.

You Want Me To Forgive What?

Sisters Linda and Janice had a fairly close relationship, and they spent many hours together—much like best friends often do. Their husbands also got along well, so the two couples went on golf outings and took vacations together and spent Sunday afternoons barbecuing in the backyard, often with their parents visiting too.

You can imagine how Linda felt when she walked into her house one day and found Janice in a passionate embrace with her husband. Getting involved with a best friend's spouse may be pretty bad in the love arena, but having an affair with a sister's husband may just be one of those unforgivable sins. (This probably falls into the same category as falling in love with a stepchild or a son's girlfriend—it spells disaster. For an example of the latter, remember the recent movie *Damage*, in which tragedy could be the only outcome.)

Janice and Linda's husband never did get together permanently, although they were free to since Linda left her marriage and Janice's husband left her too. For years, Janice pleaded with Linda to work with her to regain their closeness, but Linda couldn't forgive and forget. Again, we are dealing with an individual choice here, but I had trouble believing that Linda *should* reconcile with her sister. Yes, they are civil, and when their mother died, they worked together in helping their father. So in a sense, Linda has forgiven Janice, but that doesn't take away the fact that she was harmed by her sister's actions.

Some authorities might say that Linda is only hurting herself by not renewing a close tie with Janice. Frankly, I couldn't see that, and in fact, Linda seemed to be doing quite well. She remarried a few years after her divorce, has two children, a great career, and an active life. She simply doesn't trust her sister as a person anymore. Is there really one correct path here? I'm not convinced that there is. It's one thing to forgive and move on, but it's a far different issue to expect a relationship to return to its original closeness.

Are We Our Sibling's Keeper?

My client Marion had, on her own, set limits on how much time she spent with her competitive, jealous brother, Greg. Marion had avoided Greg because he seemed to spend most of his time picking fights, which was behavior reminiscent of their childhood. Marion knew that she was the favored child in many ways, but there wasn't anything she could do about that as an adult. Her parents, however, kept setting up situations in which the two would be thrown together. Aside from the guilt that was being put on Marion, her parents also were admonishing the two siblings to take care of each other.

In Marion's case, she knew the situation with her brother wasn't serious; she just didn't like him very much. "I'd never ignore him if he became ill or was in real trouble," she said, "but I just don't care to be around him." She shrugged her shoulders and added, "I'd never choose him as a friend."

If you find yourself in a situation in which you simply don't like to be around a particular family member, ask yourself if you'd choose this person for a friend. If the answer is no, then decide for yourself just how much time, if any, you care to spend with this sibling or cousin or aunt or uncle. Family loyalty is one thing; socializing is another.

As I said, I do advise attempting to work things out with siblings. My sister and I found that talking about the hurt and anger that had come between us helped us turn our distant relationship into a close, warm one. We share a history and we can see how much we're alike in some ways. Sometimes we laugh when we remember our mother's message: Take care of each other because there's not a man around who can do it as well. (But that's another story.)

WHOSE KID IS THAT ANYWAY?

Don and Dina have three children, the youngest of which has been a problem most of his life. Even as a young child, Jay was always in trouble at school, at scouts—and at home. Dina summed up his behavior as rude and sullen. As a teenager, Jay began abusing drugs and alcohol and his difficult behavior intensified. Fortunately, some of the professional help that Don and Dina sought for Jay led him into a chemical dependency treatment program. Eventually Jay settled down and now has a wife and son.

Unfortunately, Jay has not given up his troublesome behavior and he's been fired from a series of jobs and is always in a financial mess. After years of bailing Jay out, Don and Dina have said, "No more. We'll pay for counseling so that you can learn to solve your problems and stand on your own as an adult."

Jay, however, has a different idea. He reacted to his parents' ultimatum with anger and his most potent threat is that he will keep them from seeing their grandchild. Don and Dina came to me because they are torn apart over their difficult child, whose behavior is still a mystery to them.

I don't bring up this situation because I believe there is one solution or any easy choices. But I do believe that parents often need help with their guilt feelings when they change their behavior. They also need help with their guilt over the fact that they dislike this surly son; they may love him, but he isn't likable. So, what can they do? Sadly, they are not unique. Other people have this problem too.

Drawing Lines With Grown Children

There is probably no bond more complicated and intense than that between a parent and child. As we come to know our children as individuals, most of us feel drawn to each one as a unique person with a special ability to pull at our heartstrings as no one else can.

If we can have a child that, while perhaps not a "favorite" in the purest sense of the word, but certainly one we seem to relate to the best, why can't the opposite be true? Perhaps you have more trouble liking or getting along with the child who is exceptionally annoying or even mean. Don't misunderstand me. When a difficult child is very young, he or she may need more of your attention than your more easygoing children. You may need to extend even more of your love and affection to the child who is having trouble growing up. But, like Don and Dina, once this child is grown, parents may need to just admit that the child isn't likable.

I've seen parents of grown children relate many stories that on the face of them can only lead to anger and resentment. These situations include:

- Grown children who take parents for granted and expect them to drop everything to baby-sit, take care of the dog, or loan them money for their perpetual emergencies.
- Adult children who belittle their parents' opinions, make fun of them for being old, and put down all their ideas as old fashioned and dumb.
- Children who invade their parents' home and act as if they still live there. They don't offer to help with a meal and they react with anger if their old rooms aren't kept exactly as they were, that is, shrines to their childhood.
- Grown children who come back home and expect their parents, usually the mother, to cook for them and do their laundry. They may not even pick up after themselves.

These situations often make parents feel intense dislike for their children. They may even throw up their hands and say, "Where did we go wrong? We thought we were raising them to be nicer than they are."

Accompanying these feelings of dislike are the inevitable feelings of guilt and self-blame. We are used to thinking that everything our children do for as long as they live can be placed at our doorstep. As a result, many parents continue to put up with the unpleasant behavior and the demands, because they don't want to admit just how difficult and rude their children can be.

A friend of mine finally learned to say no, no, no, to many of her daughter's unreasonable demands, only after she saw how her grown child behaved to everyone else in the world. "It finally occurred to me," my friend said, "that if Liz could be so nice and polite to her colleagues and friends, then she could be that way to me!" A few days later, she told Liz that she would no longer baby-sit on demand and when she came to visit, she could help cook and clean up the kitchen after their meal. When Liz just laughed off her mother's comments as evidence of nothing more than having a bad day, my friend said, "You don't seem to understand—I don't like you when you are demanding and rude. I love you, but I don't like to have you around. If you can treat your coworkers and your friends with respect, you can treat me with respect too."

Liz eventually got over her snit and later said that she'd had no idea just how unreasonable she'd been. At age thirty-five, she still hadn't learned to see her parents, particularly her mother, as distinct human beings with ideas, thoughts, and feelings of their own. If my friend had not confronted her daughter, Liz might not have come to this important realization for many years, if ever. In other words, when we allow our children to treat us badly, we are not doing them a favor.

Don and Dina sorted through their feelings in therapy and concluded that they should hold firm and let their son stand on his own. While they didn't abandon him, they came to the realization that bailing him out financially had actually kept him dependent and immature.

Without question, it's possible to love your children deeply even when you find that you dislike them. If you are in this situation, take time to think about how this unpleasantness developed. If you want to change it, consider what limits you should set. Be self-protective about this. You may have to admit that your children are rude and unpleasant to you and perhaps you'll have to confront them and make some demands of your own. If you have a grown child living with you, you're not obligated to cook or clean for this adult. You have the right not to have the dog in your home for weeks and weeks. You don't have to succumb to the pressure to drop your own social life to baby-sit at a moment's notice. You have the right to say no to any demand you believe is unreasonable. Love is not the issue here, mutual respect is.

Go Ahead, Bribe and Indulge If You Want To

It's a common lament: "Now that my kids are grown, I never see them," or "My son-in-law doesn't like to spend time with us so we don't get to see our grandchildren very much." The most painful situation might be that the kids come around when they need something, but then—poof—they are gone again, maybe for months at a time.

Let's face it. We live in a mobile society and our children may scatter throughout the country. Even when they live close by, early adulthood is often taken up with establishing careers, finding a mate, having children, buying a first home, and so on. Visiting parents may be low on the list of priorities. This has nothing to do with love; still, it may be hurtful to parents. Furthermore, if sons- and daughters-in-law consider it a chore to visit, it may be in your best interest to sweeten the pot, so to speak.

My husband and I have found a solution to the busy kids syndrome that works for us, but oh how we hear about it from friends and relatives. The critics come out of the closet when they see us pay for family vacations or a restaurant meal for ten. We are also generous with gifts and money, actions which our friends call sheer bribery. "You're bribing them for love and time," they say.

Well, it may seem like bribery, but it doesn't feel like that to us. Our children still come to visit even when they aren't offered anything special. We receive much warmth and love from them, and we've never worried about being taken advantage of. We also want to see our grandchildren as much as possible. If we didn't have the money, of course, we wouldn't do it, and we don't offer gifts or trips or restaurant meals that are beyond our means.

I believe that generosity of spirit is often rewarded and even if it is "bribery" sometimes, so what? The ongoing contact might actually help in attempts to build a closer relationship with grown children. And, if your gifts are given without strings attached, even in-law children will probably learn to be comfortable with them.

Generosity or Interference?

It's important to separate gifts that are given in a spirit of respect and love and those given with a motive of control. Do you find yourself resenting that you loaned your grown children money for a house that *you* think is a monstrosity? Do you invite your children and grandchildren to share a cottage in Maine for two weeks and then criticize the way they handle their child's temper tantrums or demand that the children go to bed earlier than they're used to? After all, you generously offered these goodies, so don't you have a say in what your children do?

For the most part, unless you are not treated with respect, or your children make unreasonable demands on you, it's better to stay out of your children's lives. They have the right to decide what is right or wrong for them. Your children may love the monstrosity house. Perhaps they allow their children to stay up late because both parents work all day and they want to spend time with them. There is probably no more deadly phrase to use with grown children than, "I hope you don't mind if I tell you something..."

Grown children will often ask for your opinion, especially if they believe they will get honest answers that are devoid of subtle, or not so subtle, criticism. Your opinions, like your gifts, can then be offered with no strings attached.

My husband and I have found that there is great pleasure in giving our children gifts they really enjoy, especially because we are clear that they have the right to make decisions that we wouldn't have recommended. This is also the best way I know to form affectionate bonds with in-law children, who may be scared to death that you will interfere. So what if others call it bribery. If you aren't worried that you're buying love and attention, then you probably aren't.

WHEN IN DOUBT, THROW OUT THE BOOK

So far, we've been talking about handling problems with grown-up children. Now let's look at how many myths there are about raising infants and small children. At no other time in history have there been more "experts" to advise us as we travel along the difficult path of parenting. Unfortunately, we usually are led to believe that there is one "right" way.

My son Stephen was born thirty-two years ago, during the time that Benjamin Spock was the acknowledged "god" of baby care. My copy of his book was in tatters by the time the baby was three months old! Dr. Spock said that a baby should have fresh air every day: If the weather was too foul to allow for an outing in the baby carriage, then place him or her in front of an open window for a nap. I dutifully sat in my tiny apartment, bundled in coats and sweaters while Stephen slept on. I should have thrown away the book. (To be fair, I'm sure Dr. Spock didn't expect his readers to follow his advice so literally.)

Sometimes being a parent—especially a first-time parent—can turn an intelligent, independent, confident person into an insecure mouse. We are so afraid of making a "mistake" that we turn to the printed word for a voice of authority rather than using our own good sense to solve the problem—if there even is a real problem. It took me years to realize that my own common sense was better than any advice I received from all the authority figures I littered my life with.

So my first premise about raising children: Throw away the book. The second premise: Take advice with a healthy bunch of salt—not a grain, a handful. I once had a friend, who had not yet had children, visit me often when my own kids were young. Again and again, she told me that she would certainly do things differently when she had children. Never, never, never would she give in to her child's tantrum. What joyful revenge I felt as, years later, I watched her hand over the candy that little Jenny wanted—and was starting a tantrum to get. Like most of us, my friend was prepared to do just about anything to a avoid a public screaming scene.

I also suffered needlessly when I let my daughter sleep on a cot in our bedroom because she'd begun to be frightened while sleeping alone in her own room. Many experts said I was sure to produce a dependent, possibly neurotic child. But I'd already begun to follow my own gut and was listening to experts less and less. For many months our daughter enjoyed the security of Mom and Dad being close by and eventually she just drifted back to her own room. Today, my daughter is normal, well-adjusted, independent, and someone to be proud of. In addition, there are now experts around who actually encourage parents and small children to share the "family bed."

In recent years, my children have marveled over the many "wrong" things I did as I brought them up. Imagine, they say, it's okay not to like your sister today or share your favorite toys, and it's even okay not to eat vegetables. To be sure, I didn't throw out all the rules and I'm not suggesting that kids be allowed to do whatever they please. But I am saying that every child is different and there is no book that can possibly supply all the answers to the challenges you face when you are raising each individual, unique child.

Do Teens and Rules Mix?

As children move through their teen years and into young adulthood, we are often torn between the idea that we must clamp down and set strict rules and our intuitive sense that we must listen attentively to their concerns. We may need to let them help us solve our problems with them. Perhaps our most important job is to remain flexible enough to encourage independent decision-making on their part. We may need to let them make choices we believe are wrong, but these decisions may not be wrong for them. This is a tough period of child rearing. There's no doubt about it, especially when we have strong feelings about these "wrong" choices.

Today, parents are terrified of AIDS and therefore, are concerned about their children's sexual activities. We can make our feelings known, but we must also face the fact that we don't control this aspect of our children's lives. They may listen to us and they may ignore us, especially if we insist on certain behavior, for example, complete abstinence.

Fearful about her daughter's sexual activity, Leslie insisted that she stay at college every weekend instead of coming home so that she could be with her boyfriend. Holiday visits only was their rule. Leslie was confident that her daughter was listening and "obeying" this rule. Imagine her surprise when she ran into the girl and her boyfriend in a shopping mall. The daughter worked out her own way to be with the boyfriend, but it all took place behind her mother's back. The fact is, the young couple were responsibly sexually active. They knew about AIDS and they conducted their sex lives aware of prevention and with full knowledge of each other's sexual histories, which were minimal in their case. Leslie had no control over her daughter's choices, but it took her a long time to accept this.

Hang On With a Loose Grip

I understand that some parents have strong religious convictions about any sexual activity outside of marriage. They obviously have a right to their beliefs and they can admonish their children to abide by these rules. However, I believe it is unwise to reject or severely punish young people whose actions are contrary to these rules. If parents overreact, they may drive the children away for long periods of time. With some patience and luck, the children may return to the fold of the family's religious beliefs. And if they don't, we are still forced to let our children make their own mistakes and develop their own value system, even if it is far different from our own.

Children will often go their own way when it comes to choosing friends, picking a major in college, experimenting with different clothing and music, and deciding on a career path. In other sections of the book, we address the issue of allowing young people to "follow their own star," free from parents' insistence that they do it their way. However, no matter what issue we raise, the message is still the same: what is right for you may not be right for someone else, not even your own child.

BIRTHS, WEDDINGS, FUNERALS— OH MY!

If you want to bring out the legions of experts—amateur and professional—then try planning one of the major transition events of life. Fortunately, births can't be overly orchestrated by family members and friends, but they can try. For example, when you named your baby did folks come out of the woodwork to tell you what a stupid or silly name it was? Or did you hear about every other person with that name who did horrible things? One of my clients was told that she absolutely could not name her son Theodore because, after all, Ted Bundy was a serial killer.

Then there is the issue of showers (baby and wedding). Aunt Sue won't come because she hasn't spoken to Aunt Ruth in twenty years; your mother won't invite your step-sister, even though she's become one of your closest friends; or your father's new wife has never met your mother and everyone tells you that sparks will fly.

Over the years, I've heard about every kind of problem you can imagine arising during these major events in people's lives. And, I have also watched as clients struggled to find creative solutions to the stressful challenges that inevitably appear. One unforgettable client decided that women-only showers were outdated. She insisted that her father and two brothers, her uncles, male cousins, the man she was marrying, and all his male friends were invited to her wedding and her baby showers. You can imagine how traditionalists took to that. But, as she said, "Hey, it's my wedding and my baby." Another client canceled her wedding shower because her mother and father and their second spouses were fighting over wedding arrangements. She finally decided that it wasn't worth the hassle to even have the wedding so she and her groom eloped. (Her family learned the lesson well and settled their differences by the time a grandchild arrived.)

Our Wedding, Our Way

If you're faced with problems over these major transition events, take some comfort in knowing that you're not alone. For some reason, weddings seem to bring out the largest array of critics. The bride and groom often are manipulated into doing things they don't want because: it's always done this way; what would your grandparents think if you wear a suit instead of a white gown; we owe invitations to six hundred people so you can't have a small buffet for fifty; you must have all four sisters as bridesmaids or their feelings will be hurt. The list could go on and on. What a young couple hopes is going to be a happy event becomes increasingly stressful, and tempers flare over these details.

Nowadays, one of the most emotionally charged issues has become, of all things, the question of who will be given the honor of walking the bride down the aisle, or as it is sometimes called, "giving the bride away." One of my young clients was being torn apart by her mother's insistence that her step-father walk her down the aisle. But Michelle wanted her birth father to do it. Admittedly, he hadn't been the most attentive father in the world, and her mother and step-father were paying for much of the wedding. (She and her groom were making their own financial contribution, too.) Michelle's sensible grandmother said that it was no one's business except Michelle's and she should make her own choice. The advice columnist in their local paper said that perhaps both men could walk her down the aisle.

Another friend suggested that her mother and birth father should do it. By the time the day arrived, everyone had hurt feelings—both fathers, her father's new wife, her mother, and, of course, Michelle. She resolved the issue by not having anyone do the honor. She walked down the aisle alone and still has a bitter feeling about the way her family behaved.

Michelle certainly made the choice her own way, but I wonder if such a drastic solution would have been necessary if her two fathers had cooperated and her mother and step-mother had stayed out of it. I don't exaggerate when I say that I have seen weddings tear families apart. Some people carry out threats not to come to the wedding if some other relative from whom they are estranged is going to be there. In many situations, the best answer to these threats is, "It's your choice." Often, people back down when they realize that the bride and groom are serious about not letting petty (and not so petty) family arguments ruin their day.

Because many couples today marry later in life and have incomes of their own, the bride's parents are not necessarily expected to pay for the wedding. In these situations the parents become almost like everyone else—invited guests. Some of my clients and friends have liked this arrangement because they can nip interference in the bud. After all, they're throwing the party, they get to choose the size of the cake.

The Thoroughly Modern Bride

One of my clients balked at the idea that anyone "should give her away," since she was thirty-one, independent, and didn't like the idea of anyone "owning" her in the first place. This woman was quite knowledgeable about the source of many of the old customs and had eliminated them from her wedding in order to make it a thoroughly modern event. She and her groom were not even exchanging wedding rings, which upset the groom's parents more than the bride's (who were used to her avant garde ways). The groom's parents couldn't help but think that if she kept her birth name, didn't wear a ring, and chose to wear a pastel cocktail dress instead of a white gown, then she must not love or respect their son very much. The groom agreed with his bride on all these issues, and the future in-laws were so fond of the bride that they later agreed that their assumptions were unfounded. The wedding was a great big happy party, less stressful than many of the traditional bashes I've attended.

If you are a bride or a groom, then assume that you can make your own choices. Sure, you may want to compromise and do some things to please your families, but if you feel strongly about something, then remember that it's your wedding and you can do it your way. We live in an age of "anything goes" when it comes to vows, rings, dresses, who foots the bill, and so on. This freedom sometimes makes the arrangements more complicated, but even the most traditional weddings are stressful.

If you're a parent who has always dreamed about your child having a particular kind of wedding, remember that it's your child's event, not yours. Do you really want to add to the stress and take away from the excitement because the food isn't what you would have chosen or the music doesn't even sound like music? Far too many parents become personally invested in all the decisions and claim it is their right to make these choices because they are making a financial contribution to the event—or even paying for everything. I believe you should decide on a dollar amount that you can afford to spend and then work with the bride and groom to help them have what they want. In this area, as in so many others, generosity of spirit usually pays off.

The Final Event

While weddings and showers are supposed to be happy events, funerals are inevitably sad ones. Unfortunately, the stress surrounding the end of life may result in family squabbles. Such things as music (or the lack of it) and choice of casket can create resentments that last for decades. One family member accuses another of being cheap and still another objects to the clothes the teen-age son wore to the service. Oh dear.

If you are an adult child charged with the responsibility of carrying out the wishes of your parent, then the decisions are in your court. You have the right to make the choices and explain to others why you acted as you did. You aren't obligated to do what Uncle Ed wants—unless you want to. It isn't your fault that your father and Uncle Ed were competitive and always snarling at one another. Now Ed wants to have a "showy" funeral to prove to the world how devoted he was. Hey, this isn't your problem.

I once knew a woman who couldn't get over the fact that her brother wasn't buried in the family plot. However, her brother had chosen cremation. This woman believed that her sister-in-law was obligated to go along with long-standing family traditions, despite her brother's desire for cremation. In this case, I believe the brother's widow did the right thing. It was the wrong thing according to many family members, but frankly, the decision wasn't theirs to make.

Because we can talk more openly about death these days, many common troubles can be avoided if we have living wills and leave clear instructions about the kind of memorial service, burial, cremation, and so on, that we want. I suggest talking about this with your parents and your adult children before a crisis occurs. I've known many people who avoided ugly scenes and ongoing conflict because written instructions were left behind.

We live in a country where there are so many traditions that it's best to keep an open mind about the way these life events are handled. If you are a guest, it's your job to fit into the tradition that is being followed. I've been to many weddings and funerals that offered completely new experiences and I've found that they enriched my life. How can we possibly judge what is right or wrong for other people during these sensitive and important occasions? I'm trying to bring this open attitude to the major events that occur in my own family.

HOLIDAYS SHMOLIDAYS

You've no doubt heard that many people report becoming depressed around the winter holidays. These "holiday blues" usually start during Thanksgiving week and lift sometime around mid-January. When we consider the pressure people are under during holidays, it's a wonder we haven't declared them hazardous to our health and outlawed them.

- "You *must* go to Grandma's house for Thanksgiving dinner—she'll be devastated if you don't show up."
- "We *always* have Christmas Eve at *my* house. You'll just have to tell Betty that her parents can have Christmas Day—it has to be this way."
- "But Dad, we can't spend the first night of Hanukkah here. We have to go to Marc's house—his parents are counting on it."
- "You can't *mean* it—how could you go to Club Med for a singles week? It's *Christmas* (or Hanukkah, Thanksgiving, Easter, Passover, New Year's Day, Memorial Day, whatever)."

Families love to have traditions. That's a fact we can't avoid, nor would we want to. Traditions are lovely in many ways. We sing the same songs, eat the same food, use the same decorations in the house, and so on, year after year. Parents often become attached to having all their children around on particular days and consider them the most special. That's why I gave a variety of examples. Both religious and secular traditions often become involved, and after a particular event has been held in a certain way more than once, it can become an obligation.

The Labored Weekend

Meg's family considered Labor Day weekend at the family cottage the one, big "must attend" event. Without giving it much thought, she made arrangements to attend year in and year out. But then Ned came along and she had a chance to fly to Paris with him for the weekend. She called her mother and told her she'd made other plans for Labor Day. To hear Meg tell it, you'd have thought she'd announced that she was joining a Satanic cult. Meg was thirty-two, single, and independent, but the pressure was on. Everyone would be heartbroken if she didn't come; her nieces could talk about nothing else but seeing Aunt Meg; her father had been looking forward to seeing her all summer; her younger brother had a problem he wanted to discuss with her and would be so let down if she didn't come.

So what did Meg do? She caved in and went to the cottage. She missed an opportunity to be with the new man in her life (whom she subsequently married), and she let her family pull "tradition" on her once again. When I heard this story, the actual incident had occurred five years before, but it might as well have happened a week ago. Fortunately, Meg had used this experience as a catalyst to begin examining the way her parents had used these traditions to control her. She discussed the whole botched weekend with Ned and he helped her sort through the manipulative games her parents played. Holidays were just symbols, not the real issue. In Meg's case, she had to limit time with her family throughout the year, and it was the best decision for her.

It isn't always easy to break away from expected appearances at family holiday events. Someone is sure to be angry about it and claim you are stomping on important traditions. However, like Meg, you may need to sort through the underlying issues and come up with your own answers.

You can usually tell if, beneath the disappointment over your decision to make different plans, there is actually a deeper issue of control. For example, if Meg's mother were truly interested only in her daughter's happiness she might have said something like, "Well, of course we'll miss you, but you can't miss Paris." Instead, she threw around threats of broken hearts and letting people down. She effectively manipulated her through guilt.

Disappointment may be a perfectly legitimate reaction. Most parents are disappointed when they must share their grown children with in-laws at holiday time. Children may even travel thousands of miles to see the other set of parents. That's the way it is. It seems to me that it's fine to express regret and tell your children you wish you could see them, but ultimately, you must let them make these choices for themselves. After all, most of us know what it's like to balance the desire to see both sets of families with the realities of the time available.

Holiday Escape

Verna had never found a balance that satisfied either set of parents. She was visibly under great strain whenever the holidays came around. For years she and her husband had been eating two full dinners every Thanksgiving, and on Christmas, they were obliged to visit her mother, his mother and her new husband, his father and his new wife, and her father and her step-mother. What a mess. There they were, dragging four children all over town in order not to "break anyone's heart." After all, this one is sick and that one is alone and the other one is getting old. Verna and her husband were treated like hostages. One year, they fooled everyone and took off for Florida in a rented camper. "Best holiday we ever had," Verna said. "Too bad everyone's furious."

Chances are that Verna wouldn't have been forced into such a drastic retreat if the parents and step-parents had been more reasonable in the first place. One year the couple tried to have everyone over to their house, but that didn't work because the ex-spouses didn't want to be in the same room together. (Not everyone is able to forgive and forget.) After the blissful (considering four kids were along) week in Florida, Verna and her husband resolved that they would never again be drawn into all this family tradition nonsense. Furthermore, they are determined not to pull the same routine on their kids. I hope they remember that.

Perhaps one reason the ski resorts and tropical hotels and golf courses are so crowded during the holidays is that so many people are escaping family pressure. Some people have wisely concluded that if they can't please everyone, they'll withdraw and take vacations away from everything.

Interfaith marriages can add special strain for families during various holidays, and great understanding is required to accommodate everyone. I've seen great pain result when families will not acknowledge the religious traditions of their in-law children, or even of their own children who have adopted a different religion. Fortunately, most people are more open-minded than they used to be, perhaps because we are finally becoming used to diversity.

Sometimes we just have to accept that we can't please everyone and everyone can't please us. If you have had it with being the person who cooks Thanksgiving dinner every year, then perhaps it's time to announce, "Someone else can take the load—I'll just help out." Or maybe you and your partner get into huge arguments every time fall rolls around. Push, pull, and back again, because you both want to be with your families for a holiday and both families want you. Take some time out from arguing and see if there isn't a better answer. Maybe you can agree to alternate yearly visits, or perhaps one of your families won't be too disappointed to miss a holiday with you, because you see them more often anyway.

Nowadays, many people have found that the less elaborate the plans, the more they enjoy these special days out of the year. At June's house, going out for dinner used to be considered a cold thing to do on holidays. Only people without warm ties would do such a thing. But one year, she announced that she wanted to try it. Her schedule at work had been so tough that she couldn't face company or cooking. Her husband wasn't pleased at first, but since he didn't want to cook all day either, out to an expensive restaurant they went. The kids loved it, as June knew they would. Her mother was horrified and declined an invitation to join them (spend all that money when you could cook at home!), but June did what was right for her. She plans to do it next year as well.

Another couple bought trays of food from a supermarket for the annual New Year's day gathering at their house. Some of the relatives had the nerve to criticize them, but some people will do that even as they enjoy your hospitality.

Other people have found that using holidays as a time to be of service to others can take the focus off holiday stresses. For example, the Andersons help serve Christmas dinner in a homeless shelter located near the university where both parents teach. This family is trying to deemphasize the materialism that the holiday seems to encourage.

Like births, weddings, and funerals, holidays are here to stay. We might as well make the best of them and establish the traditions we want for ourselves, knowing that we can't force our children to want them too.

WHOSE MOTHER (OR FATHER) IS THIS ANYWAY?

Sometimes it's the children who need to back off and realize that they can't control their parents anymore than their parents can control them. Maurice is eighty-eight; Mabel is eighty-three. They are living together, and much to amazement of their children, having sex! They have never had so much fun—dancing every night, staying out late, going on senior citizen hikes. Their children are shocked at their public show of affection. Imagine this—two great-grandparents kissing in public.

Mabel and Maurice are understandably annoyed when their two sets of grown children (who are not so young themselves) insist their parents quit all this running around. In truth, they don't like the idea of their parents having sex, so they cloak their disapproval in concern—all this activity is too strenuous for such old people. Surely, they will drop dead soon. Mabel just laughed and said, "So what if I drop dead from having fun?"

There are situations, and this is one of them, when children decide they have some power and authority over their parents. They might as well see the folly of their thinking, however, and reconsider what they believe is "wrong" about their parents actions. In this case, Mabel and Maurice intend to get all the fun they can out of what they most assuredly know are their last years. "We are not going to wait around to die," they told the gathering of children and grandchildren who had come to show them the error of their ways. Good for them, I say. The children will have to adjust.

Gambling Rose

Rose wasn't waiting around to wither and die either. I didn't know her until her daughter insisted that she come in for counseling. Rose's problem, according to her daughter, was that she visits the casinos in Atlantic City twice a week or so and sometimes loses a few hundred dollars playing the slot machines. Her children were terribly worried. "She'll spend all her money there and then she'll be dependent on us. Maybe she should go to Gamblers Anonymous. The whole family is turned upside down."

I found seventy-nine-year-old Rose to be delightful and perky, with a great sense of humor. She hadn't really wanted to take time out from her busy schedule to visit me, especially when she knew herself well enough to know that she wasn't a compulsive gambler.

"I live alone, and still miss my late husband," she said, "but I stay busy with activities at the church and at the community senior center. I love Atlantic City, and when I go there I set aside a certain amount of money. If I lose it, I quit immediately, and if I win I keep on playing until I'm tired. It's my money, so what's the big deal?"

What indeed? As it turned out, Rose had a few issues that were bothering her and she came back a few times to discuss them with me. She was worried about her future and fretted sometimes about the possibility that she would one day be a physical (not financial) burden to her children. Because she had become too slow and somewhat frail, she had been asked to cut down her volunteer hours at the local hospital. This had made her sad, but the gambling trips had taken away some of the restlessness she felt.

Rose's story made perfect sense to me. She enjoyed her gambling excursions and had made some new friends during her days at the casinos; she spent only the amount of money she could afford to lose; her activities made her days fly by; and last, she found she coped with the loss of her husband better than before.

Rose's children weren't happy with my advice, at least not at first. But Rose had the right and the capacity to determine the course of her own life. There are times that we simply must let our parents go their own way.

Whose Life Is It Anyway?

My sessions with Rose made me think about my own father, who had also loved to gamble. He also liked to drink, smoke, and generally live a carefree life. Kids today would say that he was basically a party animal. At age sixty-five he was told that he had a bad heart; if he wanted to live, he'd have to change his ways. Like many people, my father tried to be "good" and he followed the doctor's advice for a time. However, it was not long before he was back to his old ways and was happier, if not healthier.

My mother and my siblings and I urged him to clean up his lifestyle so that he would live longer and we could enjoy having him around. But, my father's position was that if he couldn't enjoy life, he wouldn't be much fun to be around anyway. At age sixty-nine he died without having given up anything he loved, and we were angry with him for many years. I viewed him as selfish, but now after so many years have passed, I respect his right to choose how he wanted to live his life. It wasn't the choice our family would have preferred, but it was his conscious decision. He was clear that he wanted to fill his days with these so-called dangerous activities rather than live moderately but, in his eyes, less richly, for a longer time.

I once questioned people's right to die—especially when a person actively chose suicide. But now I wonder if it is always wrong. Maybe there are times when this "sin" is the right answer for a particular person. Certainly, it doesn't seem like the best solution, but can we always judge it as wrong?

A companion issue is the ethical dilemma involved in prolonging life when hope of recovery is gone. Most people don't want to linger and be kept alive by machines, and I believe it is their right to have a living will that expresses their wishes. Do children do themselves or their parents a favor by refusing to let go of Mom or Dad? Whose interests are being served? Death with dignity is no longer an empty phrase, because people are exploring what this concept means and making their own choices. Many people criticized author Betty Rollins when she participated in her mother's decision not to linger in pain but instead, end her own life at a time that she chose. I respect Rollins' choice, because she respected her mother's decision. She admitted that she couldn't possibly know what was best for anyone, even her own mother.

When Demands Are Too Great

"It's a sin to put a parent in a nursing home," Ben declared, his arms folded across his chest. "It's morally wrong." Jane, his older sister, was understandably upset with her brother's high and mighty attitude. After all, who faced the burden of caring for their mother? "You and Ed won't help out, and yet you're telling me I'm committing a sin," she retorted.

As a family therapist, I'd seen these arguments before. And despite all the progress women have made, there are still some men around who believe that women are the "natural" caretakers of aging parents. Ben and Ed, Jane's brothers, insisted that they were too busy and "stressed out" with their jobs and families to take care of their mother, who was recovering from a serious stroke and needed constant care.

According to their belief system, it was okay for Jane to quit her job (because she has a husband who makes a good living) and take care of their mother on a full-time basis (because she is better at that sort of thing). They were shocked when Jane demanded that they share in this job or their mother would have to go to a nursing home. She had no intention of giving up the work she loved because her brothers were hard-headed and selfish. The brothers never budged and eventually, their mother did enter a nursing home. This situation never was resolved within the family and the resentments linger.

The Toughest Decision

The decision to put a parent in a nursing home will bring critics out of the closet. I've seen it again and again. Sometimes it comes from family members; other times it comes from doctors. It may even come from neighbors and friends. The only "right" decision is to look carefully at your options and make the choice that feels right to you. I also recommend that siblings never ask of one another what they are not prepared to do themselves—it simply isn't fair for one child in the family to manage all the caretaking and make all the personal sacrifices.

Of course, I have seen situations in which a son or a daughter freely chose to do all the caretaking, without bitterness or resentment. In fact, one client said that she had never enjoyed her mother as much as during the time she spent helping her recover from serious surgery. She invited her mother into her home, much to the surprise of her siblings. They worried about the decision and even accused their sister of "being a martyr," but my client didn't feel that way at all. Fortunately, neither did her husband and children. This is another example of when the superficially wrong thing just may be right for that person in that situation.

THE GRAB BAG

In some families, the parents' money is viewed as the children's money, which is simply being held by the parents until they die. The most disturbing arguments I've seen among families are those over the elderly parents' money. One group of four grown children was greedily keeping track of their parents' accounts, always offering suggestions about how their folks could avoid taxes by turning their money over to the kids before they died. These children watched in horror as their parents spent money on vacations or new furniture. After all, in their minds, the parents were spending their money!

I didn't work with this family for very long, because I pointed out that the parents had a right to use their money the way they chose. "They can give it away or burn it if they want to," I finally said. It became clear to them that I had no intention of trying to convince their parents to spend less money. (People do seem to come to therapy for all kinds of reasons. In this case, they had no desire to explore their own lives; they wanted to manipulate their parents, and were looking for a therapist to help them. However, they knocked on the wrong door.)

Many families find themselves in chaos when money issues are raised in the context of aging parents. When Uncle Jack, age eighty-three, married Lynn, age fifty-nine, everyone in the family had something to say about it. The relatives were especially concerned that Jack was showering this "stranger" with money and gifts. Wasn't it only right that Jack save his money so he could leave it all to them? But who made up that rule? Jack loved his new wife, who was completely devoted to him; no one had the right to tell him he's wrong for making his own choices.

In another case, however, the children did have some rights. Their father began an affair with the practical nurse who was taking care of their mother at home. This nurse began to ask for "loans," five thousand dollars at a time. What's more, they weren't discreet about their affair, and the grown children knew their ailing mother was aware of it. Finally, they decided to confront their father. They took the position that he was free to do what he chose with his half of the couple's money, but he was not free to give away what belonged to their mother. Furthermore, they expected him to stop flaunting this affair in front of his wife. They were surprised when he agreed to their conditions, but in fact, he'd been feeling a bit guilty about his behavior.

Eventually, their mother died and the nurse is still in the picture. But the mother's estate was protected. These children could have ignored the problem, or they could have demanded that he fire the nurse and get the money back. (The latter was considered the "right" choice by many other family members and friends.) However, they would have ended up completely alienated from their father and their mother's last years would have been even more difficult. They didn't like the solution they settled for, but it was the best they could do under the circumstances and they managed to adjust to it.

When it comes to grown children and their concerns for their parents, let's keep in mind the old story about the man whose wife died and the next day, the children were in the house, ready to carry out her jewelry, clothes, and anything else that pleased them. "Hold on," he said, "I want these things." The children then accused him being selfish. This kind of story is so common that comedians having been making a living on it for centuries.

PUTTING IT ALL TOGETHER

As I said in the beginning, relationships with family members are about as complex as life gets. Advice, from any source, needs to be taken with many grains of salt. After years of working with clients, I'm convinced that none of us can expect to be happy if we try to fit all our decisions into the mold of convention. Yes, try to work things out, make concessions if they feel right, but in the end, resolve family issues in your own way.

SEVEN

Money, Careers, and Lifestyles

When I was a young mother and homemaker I was often asked, "And what do you do?" My usual reply was, "Nothing—I just stay home with the kids." That was a long time ago, during the days when just about anything a woman did was considered less valuable than the pursuits of men. At the time, I didn't understand that my job was at least as important as my husband's. But then, few women saw the role of homemaker as equal in value to that of breadwinner.

Some things change; some don't. In our society, the kind of work we do still defines us to an extent. "What do you do?" is often the first question we ask a person we've just met. While this isn't necessarily wrong, it is a reflection of our tendency to give (or withdraw) varying levels of respect based on what people do (or don't do) for a living. As a result, some people choose careers that are prestigious, even if they aren't particularly suited for that line of work.

In a similar way, we form values about money and financial success. Some people, and I was once such a person, can't spend money they have because they fear it will disappear one day. For example, as a child I learned that "a penny saved is a penny earned," and my mother would walk blocks out of her way to save a few cents on the groceries. Since we were quite poor, I don't fault her. She did what she had to do. However, frugality was so instilled in me that even as I became more financially comfortable in my life, I still had difficulty spending money, especially on myself. I gradually changed my attitudes and learned to make different choices regarding money. How many times have we heard about a supposedly impoverished elderly person who dies with millions stashed in the mattress? I didn't want to be that kind of person.

No one escapes acquiring attitudes about money, careers, and certain kinds of lifestyles—yet so often we enter our adult lives without being completely conscious about where and how we picked up these attitudes. As our lives and circumstances change, we would do well to examine these attitudes and decide if they still work for us today. As you read through the following examples, notice your reactions to each situation. Do your reactions reflect some beliefs and attitudes that you hold?

STRIVING FOR THE MIDDLE GROUND

Charles, a dentist, is married to Traci; they have two little girls. He likes to work during the day only, and at five o'clock head home to spend time with his family. This sounds fine, but Traci was pressuring Charles to keep his office open a few evenings a week so he could see more patients and make more money. Both their families agreed with Traci. In addition to the financial issue, the concept of the "work ethic" was also raised. In other words, even Charles' family thought that his nine-to-five attitude meant that he wasn't willing to "work hard" for his family.

Traci and Charles decided to seek counseling because this problem was eroding their relationship. Traci had difficulty understanding that Charles simply hadn't bought into the notion that his job was to make as much money as he could, regardless of how much time it took. She interpreted his attitude as laziness, and how could she approve of a lazy husband? However, once they had improved their communication, Traci began to see that laziness wasn't the issue. In fact, she began to understand that her husband was trying very hard to be a good "family man," which meant that making a lot of money didn't have the highest value in his eyes. To him, devotion to his family involved spending time with them, not making all the money he possibly could.

Charles and Traci illustrate a situation that is becoming quite common. You may have found yourself having some reactions to their story, which reflects some new ways of looking at family life and the role expectations for men and women. For example, many people would agree with Charles, and if they had a chance to tell Traci what they think, they might say, "If you want money for more luxuries, wait until your children are older and go out and work for them yourself." Some men might envy Charles his profession—after all, he can make a good living working for himself and setting his own hours. Still others might be suspicious about his unwillingness to provide even more money for his family.

A few decades ago, it would have been unthinkable for a man to pass up a promotion because he wanted to spend more time with his wife and kids. Yet I see this happening more and more. Men are giving up their jobs because their wives have been transferred; many women turn out to be more ambitious than their partners. As I see it, being ambitious might be right for some people, but wrong for others.

Dad Stays Home and Likes It

In chapter 3, I described a situation in which a father decided to stay home and be the homemaker in the family, but it didn't work out for that couple. However, it sometimes works very well, especially if the people involved sort through their attitudes about unconventional lifestyles.

Karen and Bill are in their thirties, have been married for thirteen years, and have three children. Karen, a successful lawyer, works long hours; Bill, once a mid-level manager at a small manufacturing company, gave up his job to stay home and manage the household. He does most of the cooking and cleaning, and oversees the children's school activities. By all accounts, he runs a comfortable and efficient household.

This couple came to me for counseling because they found themselves arguing about money, chores, and how to spend free time. In addition, they were having trouble coping with all the criticism thrown their way by family and friends. Karen's parents had recently expressed their anger at Bill, who they judged as lazy and not a real man (whatever that is). I could see that Karen and Bill really loved each other and wanted their marriage to work. Since they both were happy with their respective roles, they had decided that Bill should not seek a job outside their home at this time. It seemed to me that they needed to solve all the other kinds of problems most couples have. However, they had the added difficulty of getting parents and friends off their backs. They had been belittled for so long that they needed affirmation that their choice was okay for them.

Karen and Bill worked it out, and they became part of a growing number of couples who choose unconventional lifestyles. Their concerns also expose the lie we have perpetuated: Men are valued for the work they do, and homemaking is not considered work. Supposedly, it's a woman's job, and men often give lipservice about how difficult it is. Karen would not have been considered lazy had she decided to be the homemaker. However, it wouldn't be assigned too much value either. What a pity. How strange it is that cleaning house and tending children is given even minimal respect only if women do it. When men enter the domestic arena, the work is considered beneath them and they aren't "real men" if they willingly do it. Like many women, I've spent time as a homemaker and as a career woman, and on balance, homemakers have the tougher job in many ways.

We still hear the term "role reversal" applied to a situation like Karen's and Bill's, but eventually, that term will probably fade away. Gender roles are so fluid now (and becoming more so) that expectations about what men and women are "supposed to do" are rapidly disappearing. However, young couples today are caught in this transition, which can lead to misunderstandings between them and frowns of disapproval from family and friends. You might want to examine your attitudes and values in this area and determine if you still carry around some old definitions about sex roles and what so-called real men and women are supposed to do. As many of my clients have found, these definitions often do a disservice to individual men and women.

Refusing to Climb the Ladder

Tom, like Charles, is another individual who likes to keep his work as free of stress and strain as possible—he's too busy living the rest of his life to worry about climbing the traditional ladder to success. Tom works as a counselor in a home for the elderly and has consistently refused offers to become a supervisor. From his perspective, his coworkers have become friends, and he doesn't wish to become an authority figure who's in charge of them.

At one point, Tom was given only a few days to make a decision about accepting or refusing a promotion. Despite urging from family and friends, he did his own soul searching and was comfortable with his decision to stay at the same professional level. While our society generally values the concept of upward mobility, Tom had the courage to say no.

Money or Magic?

Buddy and Lila, friends of mine, are one of the most delightful couples I've ever known. However, their families don't think highly of them because Buddy makes his living as a magician and Lila makes hers as a psychic reader. They often work together at parties, although each also has a separate clientele.

Buddy started his career in magic as a small child and by the time he was a teenager, he was making extra money as a magician at children's parties. His family thought this was a terrific way to earn money for college, and he managed to put himself through engineering school by working conventions and parties. But everyone certainly expected that Buddy would get a real job and settle down eventually.

Buddy also believed that he would probably need to give up the magic business for something more respectable and stable. But that was before he met Lila. Lila believes in her heart that people should do what they love and what they do best. Her psychic abilities were appreciated in her family, so she was encouraged to celebrate her special skill—and if that meant others thought she was eccentric, then so be it.

Needless to say, Buddy's family wishes that Lila had never appeared. "If only Buddy hadn't met Lila," they say, "he would be a successful engineer today." Instead, Lila and Buddy live in a little house, much smaller than his family approves of, and they both have become successful at their unconventional occupations. Each could be making more money at other professions, but this couple appears not to need all the trappings so many other people require in order to be happy. I often think that if more people had the happiness and generosity of spirit that this couple has, the world would be a more gentle, peaceful place.

YOU MAY HAVE MORE OPTIONS THAN YOU KNOW

If you are not happy in your work life, and you can find some way to change it, then go for it. This may mean changing jobs more often than is considered wise; it may mean doing something entirely out of the ordinary; it may mean starting a business that ultimately fails. You may be called a slouch or a failure by family members, and friends may shake their heads in confusion as you start another job or refuse promotions. Or, like Paul, the son of a friend of mine, you might work part time and live modestly while you're writing a novel or maybe building a boat in your backyard.

Sometimes I sense envy on the part of those who do all the head shaking and eyebrow raising. I certainly saw this in Paul's case. He was working as a part-time security guard while he wrote novels and plays. His family was alarmed by his unwillingness to get a professional job, but a few cousins openly expressed their envy about his ability to go after his dream. At family gatherings, these cousins would often defend Paul and speak of his courage.

The fact is, Paul doesn't mind sharing an apartment with two other young men, or eating plain vegetarian fare, or even buying his clothes at thrift shops. He's accepted responsibility for himself, so whose business is it what he does? This would be a far different situation if the thirty-five-year-old Paul was asking his parents or other relatives to support him. But he isn't; he takes care of himself and his own needs.

Let me stress here that I'm not suggesting there is anything wrong with following a conventional career path, nor am I advocating putting one's family at risk in order to find the perfect work life. I just want to caution people not to get hooked into the myth that they must stick to something because it's "wrong" to keep changing jobs, or it's not good to settle for less, or to work less, or—like Max—not at all.

Max had worked hard as a young man, and was considered a rising star in the sales department of an insurance company. But when he inherited millions of dollars after his father died, he quit his job and no longer works, even though he's only thirty-nine. Most of his friends say that he doesn't do anything. However, in reality, he does a lot and lives his life in a rather disciplined way. He reads a great deal, has a showpiece garden that takes much of his time, and keeps fit through a variety of sports. I say good for Max. He hasn't bought into the myth that people must either work or be considered bums. Many of us would make a different choice, but Max's decision has worked well for him.

Going After It All

Nancy and Greg are one of the most unusual couples I know. They have never hesitated to go after the things in life that are important to them. Married in their forties, they each brought children to the marriage, but they wanted more. Despite disapproval from their families, they had three children together. They also decided that Greg should go after his dream of becoming a doctor. This seemed incongruous, not just because of his age, but because Greg and Nancy always want the best—the best schools for the children, the best restaurants, the best vacations, and so forth. Going to medical school meant financial hardship, but they went after it anyway.

I'm still puzzled by the way they were able to accomplish these feats and still maintain something close to the lifestyle they were accustomed to. I know they were under enormous stress a lot of the time, but they just kept going. Predictably, their families thought they were foolish to keep on paying expensive school tuition and buying expensive clothes. I've always marveled at the way Nancy gets her regular massage even if the coffers are empty. She says that massage eases her stress, and then, more relaxed, she can think of ways to stretch the money and pay the electric bill. Today, after enduring the grind of medical school and internship, Greg is a doctor in a thriving family practice. I'm still amazed. But I respect the way they decided to live their lives in their own way, and let the criticism fall where it may.

GO AHEAD, ENJOY ALL THAT MONEY

When I first saw Rebecca, I observed a bright, attractive, pleasant young woman who was a top student at a top college. She came to me because she suffered from, as she put it, low self-esteem. It turned out that Rebecca had been born with the proverbial silver spoon in her mouth. Her affluent parents provided her with everything money could buy and were attentive, caring parents as well.

Instead of having the confidence that such a privileged individual might have, she was consumed with many fears about her ability to take care of herself. She believed that she would never know how to make it on her own and was even afraid to drive her car. As she continued to see me, she also revealed that she never asserted herself with her friends because she thought she ought to let them have their own way in everything—after all, they were less fortunate. She now was hiding her expensive clothes and attempting to make herself look plain so she wouldn't stand out in a crowd.

Rebecca was in counseling with me for a long time and we explored many areas of her life, but one of the most important things she accomplished was to accept the privileges she'd been born with. She had wasted so much energy feeling guilty about her money that she'd neglected the ways in which she could learn to be independent and take care of her own needs. (Rebecca's parents encouraged her to find work she loved and to build her own life; they simply didn't want her to be unnecessarily deprived in the process.)

Eventually, Rebecca discovered how truly capable she was. Although only twenty, she had a multitude of accomplishments. For example, she was an excellent pianist, had spent many hours as a volunteer at a center for disabled children, her grades had always been high because she was so well organized, and in most situations, people took a liking to her. She imagined that they saw the money, but in actuality, she found that many of her friends didn't even know about her privileged life and those who did, didn't care. Sure, there were some jealous people who would never like Rebecca because they resented her. However, she learned to ignore them and focus on the positive things and people in her life. (This was a very long process. Rebecca had to give herself credit for many things before she could be comfortable with her affluence.)

Like many people from privileged backgrounds, Rebecca decided to work at a job that enables her to help people less fortunate. Now she realizes the money she has at her disposal can help her realize that goal. In other words, she sees the money as a way to open the door to meaningful things.

It's often been said that no one is ever successful alone; successful people always had help. Perhaps the disadvantaged person credits a teacher or a counselor or a role model for inspiring him or her. If another person has money and the advantages it brings, why shouldn't he or she accept that form of help too?

As much as we like to say that we live in a classless society, the fact is, we don't. Some people will always get the best table because their relatives own the restaurant (or the whole block) and some people simply don't have to wait for the bus because they can afford to take taxis. Still others don't have to worry about hailing taxis because they have a limo.

Enjoying privilege and affluence is not the same as flaunting it, or otherwise using it in a negative way—no one likes an arrogant braggart. Arnie is such a man. He is the boss's son, so he never bothered to learn the skills necessary to hold the number two job in the company. He spends his work hours being obnoxious to employees as he bosses them around and belittles their work. He shows off each new purchase and brags about his private airplane. Not surprisingly, he has managed to earn several ugly nicknames. Meanwhile, he's running the company into the ground because of his incompetence. Even Arnie's mother finds him insufferable and wonders what they can do to change him. Some people might consider it "wrong," but Arnie's mother is urging his father to fire him. That seems right to me.

Why Aren't They More Like Us?

- They live too high!
- They're so cheap.
- They live like pigs.

- They never go out.
- They're always away from their children.
- They take too many vacations.
- They have too many pets.
- They wear jeans to the opera.
- They aren't normal—they're gay.
- They aren't normal—they don't work hard.
- They aren't normal—they practice a weird religion.

And so it goes...on and on. There will always be someone who criticizes the way you live. Feed your kids beans and rice and someone will tell you they should have burgers—for protein, you know. Feed your kids burgers and someone will tell you you're ruining their health—too much fat, you know. Limit your social life so you can strive to succeed in your career and people will call you a workaholic; take an easy job to reduce stress and to give you time for a social life, and people will call you lazy. Face it, you can't win if you're looking to others for approval of what you do.

DID HE BLOW THE WHISTLE— OR JUST BLOW IT?

It took Bernie a long time to rise in the company and now he's the chief engineer on a sensitive technical project. But Bernie learned that the project was being compromised by shortcuts and falsified test results. If the proposed product were to be released, lives could be endangered. Bernie lived with his secret at work, but at home he confided in his wife, who unfortunately, worked for the same company. They wrestled with the problem together, debating what to do.

Finally Bernie went to the chief manager of his department and told him what knew. What a relief! Two days later, Bernie was fired, and then he was accused of company sabotage. Bernie's wife, Carla, was fired on the same day. If this all sounds fantastic, just watch some of the magazine programs on television. This situation isn't so rare.

You probably can guess the rest. Bernie and Carla had no jobs and no money. They managed to find a lawyer who would work on a contingency basis and a short time later, they filed a suit against the company. They went to the local press and told their story, and now the whistle blowing is complete. Reactions among family and friends are mixed. Some agree with Bernie and Carla and call them courageous; others think they should have looked the other way and kept quiet because they have young children. In other words, they should have done the ethically wrong thing because it's more important—right—to take care of one's family first.

It will no doubt take years for the legal issues to be resolved and Carla and Bernie are struggling along, with some help from a few sympathetic relatives. They have part-time, minimum wage jobs, no health insurance, and are barely making their house payments. But their one satisfaction is that the product is not being released; the combination of the lawsuit and press inquiries have delayed it.

What do you think? Is it worthwhile to blow the whistle when you believe something unethical is occurring? Should they have kept quiet? Right now, Bernie and Carla waffle from day to day. There are times that Bernie wishes he'd quit and found another job; at other times, he believes he's doing what had to be done and that his action may have saved lives. Even he isn't certain if he was the "fool" his brother called him or the "hero" his sister says he is. What would you have done in Bernie's place? If you were Carla, what would you have advised him to do?

Gay and Proud

We only have to look at the evidence before us to see that some people live a lifestyle that's not right for them. However, they feel forced into to it by conventional attitudes, and in some cases, moral injunction.

Mary and Joan are lesbians who live together and are raising Mary's children from a former marriage. They are not upset about being gay, nor are they embarrassed. However, the neighbors have been openly hostile to them, which has caused the children an undue amount of stress. Not satisfied with merely criticizing, some of the neighbors have threatened to cause still more trouble by turning Mary and Joan in to the child welfare department. They claim this is an unhealthy situation, one that constitutes abuse. According to these busybodies, merely being raised by lesbians is abusive to the children.

Right now, Mary and Joan are considering a move to another neighborhood, even though they are happy with their present location and the schools the area offers. Fortunately, they have the support of other women in similar situations, but it isn't enough. They've had to consult a lawyer to determine how much power these neighbors have. They've also had to keep Mary's children inside the house so that one particularly preachy person can't constantly lecture the youngsters about the sin and depravity their mother and her friend are engaging in.

Recent law suits give these two women little comfort and they may be better off searching for a new environment. How sad—two fine women are subjected to harassment over their private lives, which are no one's business anyway. But, as Joan pointed out, years ago they wouldn't even have considered living together openly; they would have remained "in the closet," always worried about being found out.

Be Fruitful and Multiply—Don't You Dare

Sandy and Leon have nine children. Leon's teaching job doesn't pay well and they do struggle to make ends meets. I worked with this family when I was helping one of their sons with some emotional difficulties. At one time, nine children would have been considered a big family, but nonetheless, okay. Today,

Sandy and Leon find themselves criticized from all sides. Some people believe they have brought too many children into an already overpopulated world. Others think that Sandy and Leon can't provide enough material things—or attention—to go around. The fact is, the family is relatively happy and once the children are here, should we wish them away? Whose business is it, anyway?

In contrast, Betty and Nick are an affluent couple in their thirties, the kind of couple people label "yuppies." They don't have any children and don't plan to. They are accused of being selfish, self-centered, self-indulgent, hedonistic, narcissistic, and furthermore, they are depriving their parents of grandchildren.

Since when is it a grown child's obligation to provide grandchildren for their parents? Unwanted children are unwanted children, whether they're born into affluence or into poverty. Generations ago, people had little choice about having children; it simply went with the territory of marriage. Things have changed, and some people don't like the idea that couples can make their own choice to not have children. Critics are especially vocal if the couple is affluent, ambitious, and attractive.

Perhaps it is difficult for some parents to understand that their own children don't have the urge to become parents. They may even believe they did something wrong, but their defensive attitude is hurtful and rejecting. Perhaps the parents need to find another outlet that will satisfy their desire to be around young children. An older woman I know entered a foster grandparent program to satisfy her own desire to nurture another generation. This enabled her to stop pestering her daughter about having children.

They Just Can't Get It Together—Says Who?

Jake and Sarah live in a communal house in the middle of an urban neighborhood. They've been there for more than twenty years, so you'd think that their parents would have accepted it by now. Both are creative artists who are quite successful in their difficult fields, probably because their expenses are less than that of couples living more conventionally. They share household responsibilities with their ten housemates, most of whom are part of the original group. While many, if not most, communal situations fail for a variety of reasons, this living arrangement seems to have fostered a sense of belonging and a commitment to working out problems by using nonconfrontational methods. Jake's father calls this "wimping out," while Sarah's mother scoffs at these grown-up "hippies." Neither set of parents likes the idea that their two grandchildren were raised in this environment, but they admit that the children are marvelous—smart, generous, polite, and college bound.

I don't know Jake and Sarah, but something tells me that if their marriage and living arrangements have survived for more than two decades, they're doing something right, even if it's "wrong." Conventional wisdom tells us that the so-called "alternative lifestyles" can't last because they're too idealistic, or they're morally wrong, or inherently unstable, and so forth. But there are a growing number of Jakes and Sarahs who are looking for ways to strengthen community ties through cooperative housing, communes, buying land as a group, and many other means.

Just watch. They'll be criticized for everything they do, even as they experiment with ways to improve their communities. They'll be called wrong, wrong, wrong, but perhaps they'll be doing something that's right for themselves and others.

My God!

Almost every religious tradition has one thing in common—an unwavering conviction that its own beliefs are the only correct ones. So heaven help us in our pluralistic society, where we must all live together in a spirit of tolerance. When the tolerance breaks down, ugly consequences usually result. Religion is very personal, but it can also be considered part of a lifestyle decision.

With few notable exceptions, most religious groups are benign in the sense that they don't engage in excessive brainwashing or take their converts as hostages. Most religious groups blend into society, and usually, threats to impose beliefs on others can be handled through mediation or through our courts.

I once counseled a brother and sister who were concerned about their parents' newfound religious fervor. These middle-aged parents had stopped going to the movies, had removed alcohol from their home, were going to church several nights a week, and were participating in large conventions and conferences sponsored by the religious group. They were not, however, forcing the religion on their children, giving away all their money to this church, or otherwise engaging in anything harmful.

This situation isn't easy for children, parents, and friends. While it might look wrong, it apparently was the right thing for this set of parents. The two children ended up working on accepting their parents, rather than attempting to stop them from practicing this particular religion. Obviously, if their parents had begun proselytizing, they would have needed to draw some boundary lines, but this wasn't the case.

I've also seen Christian and Jewish parents become quite upset when their son or daughter began practicing Buddhist or Hindu meditation and attending retreats with others following a similar path. However, there are no guarantees that the religion we raise our children in will be the religion they choose later on. In most of these cases, the children are respectful of their parents' religion, and do not withdraw from the family because they have different spiritual practices. In fact, given the inclusive nature of many of these Eastern religions, most people still participate in the cultural rituals of Christianity or Judaism. This helps to keep peace in the family.

On the other hand, I understand parents' concerns when their grown children are involved with what seems to be a cult. I advise parents to learn all they can about the group, keep track of the children as much as possible, and be aware of any attempt to isolate the young people from their families. I've known of parents who have successfully removed their children from these cult-like environments. I've also observed situations in which the children left the groups on their own when pressure from their parents lessened. These parents must search their own minds and hearts in order to decide what is right for them. Of course, those who left their children alone were criticized for that; those who went after their children were condemned as control freaks. You have to do what you believe is best under the circumstances and ignore the chorus of critics.

It can't be emphasized enough that our society is becoming more complex and varied. The traditions we are accustomed to are not the only traditions we'll be exposed to in our lives. To me, this makes our culture richer and even more fun, but I know that many individuals have a difficult time adjusting to such changes. It may be the wrong thing for you to expand your horizons and explore new traditions, or it may be the right thing. Still, my basic premise stands: it's up to you, just as it's up to others to make their choices.

HOW LUCKY WE ARE

Careers, money, parenthood, sexual preference, religion, and other lifestyle issues are so complex because, in our society, we have such a wide range of possibilities open to us. Just think how lucky we are! No one can impose a certain kind of job on us. No one can tell us that we must have children (or how many and when we must have them). We are free to enjoy the money we earn and we can choose (within reason) to make more money, or to cut back our work life and live on less. In the last decade, gay people have had less need to hide. Though no longer condemned to the closet, their lives are still difficult in many ways, because, in some quarters, there is well-organized opposition to their lifestyle. However, without question, for these individuals a homosexual orientation, the so-called wrong thing, is very right. In fact, the traditional right thing is so wrong that lives have been destroyed by vain attempts to fit into the heterosexual lifestyle.

Take time to examine the lifestyle decisions you've made. Are you satisfied with them? Were the choices truly your own, or are you living in a way that feels as if something is being imposed on you? How would you like your life to be? What can you do to make a new decision if the old one just isn't right for you?

Eight

Judging "Books" By Their Covers

In our society, "packaging"—how we look, dress, talk, and live—are subject to stereotyping from all sides. A woman who has plastic surgery may be considered shallow by her neighbors, who often either can't afford the surgery or may have been blessed with good skin. Sure, they're in a position to criticize. Or how about the fifty-year-old man who still has long hair and now has added an earring? He's accused of "hanging on to his youth." But maybe the men pointing fingers are bald and jealous—who knows? Rest assured, no matter what you do with your appearance, someone, somewhere, will make negative comments about you. This is especially true if you like to experiment with clothes and makeup or deliberately attempt to look a bit different.

In this chapter, you'll have a chance to examine the way you have made decisions about how you look, how you dress, your body image, and what material things you choose to surround yourself with. Perhaps you'll find, like some of the people in this chapter, that you haven't made these decisions independent of outside influences.

MAYBE FAT IS IN

Evelyn and Tina suffered from the so-called yo-yo syndrome for years. They tried every diet imaginable, from high protein/low carbohydrate, to strict calorie counting, to liquid fasts. They'd lose pounds for a while and then, sometimes slowly, sometimes quickly, they'd gain the weight back—plus a few more pounds.

Both women were discouraged about dieting but they were also in great pain over their appearance. They came to my body image group to sort out their feelings and try to decide what to do about their weight problems. Evelyn and Tina quickly recognized that their lifelong struggle with weight had consumed so much energy that other areas in their lives were not addressed.

My work with these two women, and others like them, involved helping them accept themselves as people, not just bodies. Because of efforts on the part of many overweight people, there is increasing support for those who don't fit into the definition of "average" or "normal." Nowadays, there is a focus on acceptance and "big is beautiful." There also is a growing emphasis on marketing attractive, fashionable larger-size clothing; some magazines even use large-size models.

The two women made different choices about their appearance issues. On the one hand, Evelyn was not willing to accept her body weight, but as she became more accepting of herself and more comfortable with her appearance, she was able to use food less and less as a source of comfort. Over time, she lost some of the excess weight and began to feel more confident. She slowly enriched her life, made many new friends, and eventually changed careers.

Tina, however, gradually embraced the "big is beautiful" idea and decided she would never again attempt to lose weight. Instead, she became a spokesperson for the overweight. In the process, her personality blossomed and she became outgoing and friendly. She no longer avoided certain people and places, and eventually, she formed a support group of her own. When I last saw Tina, her calendar was filled with public speaking engagements and she was looking great in her fashionable, large-size clothes.

Both women created new lives for themselves, and both made decisions in their own way, based on what they wanted at the time. If you've been spending energy being miserable about your body, it's a good idea to forget about physical changes for a period of time. Try to find out if you can accept yourself just as you are.

Obviously, we can't ignore health concerns, and if you've been advised to lose weight immediately, then you must address this problem. Remember, too, that there are fitness programs designed for overweight people—and carrying extra pounds does not mean that you have to be a couch potato. However, even if you must follow a specific diet, self-acceptance remains an important component in expanding your life. Nothing is more sad than people who have hidden their talents and stopped growing because they have never accepted themselves as they are.

We tend to think that body image problems affect only those who are fat in this thin-worshipping culture. However, I've seen short men struggle to overcome feelings of inferiority, small-breasted women hide in lose clothing and obsess about implants, and tall women slouch to look shorter than the men they're with. Short women are given tips to look taller and thin people are urged to add pounds. Everywhere we look, body image reigns supreme. It's a wonder we have any time at all to develop our minds and hearts.

VAIN AND HAPPY

We're often judged by our bodies and our looks, yet we're also told not to be *too* vain. Sometimes an overweight person will begin attempting to look attractive, and then well-meaning friends and family members tell him or her not to be so vain.

There's definately a balance between accepting ourselves as we are and adding certain touches that make us feel good. This balance isn't always easy to achieve, especially if we listen to the opinions of others.

Myra had wanted to get a face-lift for several years and finally she was all set up to have it done. She had a problem, however, with people who couldn't stop telling her how vain they thought she was. In truth, Myra felt a twinge of guilt about indulging this desire to look younger. After all, she said, inner qualities are more important than how one looks. She also was a feminist who believed that women's looks had been emphasized far too much. Yet Myra, who was an attractive woman with a girlish, slim figure took genuine pleasure in looking good in her fashionable clothes.

When Myra sorted through all her feelings, she still wanted the face-lift. What she really needed was help in accepting the concept that it's okay to be vain. As she talked about her friends and their nasty comments, she realized that most of them dyed their hair to hide the gray and many followed strict diets and fitness programs in an attempt to stay slim. She roared with laughter as she recalled that her friend Nick had lost his hairpiece in the hot tub.

Sure, having plastic surgery is more drastic than applying hair dye or choosing a new diet or covering bald spots with a hairpiece. But the motivation is basically the same—vanity.

Depending on the messages you received when you were young, you may automatically react negatively to the mere suggestion that vanity can be a good thing. And you may have a preconceived notion about how much vanity is acceptable, and where the line simply must be drawn. Before you judge your own actions or those of others, take some time to examine your attitudes about vanity and how you acquired them. Perhaps you've been wanting to do something to enhance your appearance, but fear of being called vain has stopped you. Whose voice is it that accuses you? Sort through the conflicting messages and then do what's right for you.

Reasons Are Important

If you're considering a radical body change, such as plastic surgery or a hair transplant or even committing to a rigid diet, it's important to explore the reasons why you want to make this change. There may be underlying problems that won't be solved by changing your physical appearance, so counseling may be more effective than the change. For example, some people successfully lose weight, only to find that they are terrified of being thin. The weight was serving an important purpose, and until they understand that, they'll continue roller coaster dieting.

This is not to say that there aren't many emotionally healthy people who just like to look better, younger, or different. The desire to change something about one's appearance is not by definition a sign of insecurity, inferiority, or some other underlying emotional disturbance. Far too often, it's viewed this way, while at the same time, media messages urge us to improve ourselves. So we're set up to have conflicting feelings.

Sometimes individuals who have an emotional problem find they're able to overcome it more easily if they don't have to contend with a physical feature that is unappealing to them. Beth, for instance, was a shy, lonely girl who believed her over-sized nose made her stand out in a crowd. A plastic surgeon changed her nose to a shape and size more suitable to her face and she felt much more comfortable in public. In this case, plastic surgery literally changed her life, and today Beth has overcome her shyness and is enjoying a normal life.

Although plastic surgeons are duty-bound to warn their patients about having expectations that are too high, doctors can sometimes be wrong. Years ago, I knew a woman named Helen, who had lived life by all the rules she was taught as a child. She had been a conscientious corporate wife, a stay-at-home mother, and a volunteer in her community. Then, when she was fifty-two, her handsome husband ran off with a much younger woman. Helen was devastated, and absolutely convinced that her life was over unless she found another man to take care of her.

As part of the divorce settlement, Helen demanded money for plastic surgery. She believed in her heart that the surgery was necessary to help her make her way in the world. The surgeon was disturbed by her insistence that life was going to be just fine once the surgery was done. But, for Helen, that's exactly what happened. Her life changed in ways that went far beyond the initial plan to find another man. Newly confident about her appearance, she gradually recovered from the sadness and rage over her divorce. She developed a career of her own, traveled with friends, and changed her attitudes about dozens of things. Although she ultimately did meet a man she liked, she no longer believed she needed him to make her complete. She still maintains that the surgery was the first step in recovering from her husband's abandonment. Eventually, she wrote a letter to the surgeon that explained why, for her, life did drastically change.

ENJOYING EXCEPTIONAL BEAUTY

Susan was in her late thirties by the time she learned that it was okay to be vain and okay to enjoy her gift of exceptional beauty. She knew she was lovely, but she also felt guilty about it. She was raised to believe that vanity was a *sin*, and furthermore, that beauty and brains don't go together. Susan worked for a large corporation and was confused by all the mixed messages turning around in her head. The successful, intelligent women she worked with were openly concerned about their appearance and didn't seem uncomfortable at all with their makeup and smart clothes. But Susan had been taught that makeup would make her cheap and clothes should be plain and practical.

Once again, I saw a person who was a slave to an authority that no longer fit. She had long since abandoned the restrictive rules she was raised with, but the old messages remained. It wasn't easy for Susan to enjoy her beauty and believe that she could be both attractive and smart. She did change her clothing style and began to enjoy wearing a small amount of makeup, which enhanced her looks. Little by little, she's learning to look at her beauty as a gift.

We've all seen examples of people who are confident and seem to enjoy whatever degree of beauty they have. People like being around them, and many seem more attractive than they actually are because they feel good about themselves. And certainly, there is truth to the idea that attractiveness is in the eye of the beholder. No one is going to be considered good-looking in everyone's eyes. It's just not possible.

I've known a few people who believed themselves to be so much more attractive than others that they developed a kind of complex over it. For example, if someone didn't like Cynthia, she declared, "It's because I'm pretty *and* accomplished. She (a new acquaintance who didn't take to her) can't handle it and she's jealous." If a man didn't ask her out twice, she believed it was because she was *too* attractive. It never occurred to her that the man might not have liked her very much or that he didn't find her physically appealing. "He wants a bimbo—I threaten him," she'd say.

The fact is, Cynthia had to work on her abrasive, demanding personality in order to find close friends. She used her good looks in such a negative way that she drove people away. She is an attractive woman to be sure, but she'd also tied her looks to everything that ever happened to her. As a result, many people found her difficult to be around and she blamed their discomfort on jealousy. Until she saw herself more realistically she couldn't enjoy her accomplishments, her looks, or other people. While it was right for Cynthia to enjoy her looks, it was wrong for her to use this issue as an excuse for her social failures.

DO CLOTHES MAKE THE MAN OR WOMAN?

When Eric, a fifty-eight-year-old widower, met Hillary, age twenty-seven, she encouraged him to throw away his old, conservative suits and ties. Now he lives in jeans and even sports a ponytail, something he secretly always wanted to try. Not surprisingly, when Eric brought Hillary to his daughter's wedding, every tongue wagged: Eric is a fool; Eric is being *indecent*, running around with such a young woman; Eric is looking for his lost youth; Eric will die of a heart attack if he does that crazy dance again.

Eric just let them talk. Maybe it would be wrong for these critical folks to look and act the way Eric does, but it was the right thing for him. In fact, his daughter later commented that he'd never seemed so relaxed and content. She'd long been concerned about how lonely and unhappy he'd seemed before he met Hillary. Now she enjoys watching him become so enthusiastic about life. (Granted, not every grown-up child would be so generous.) What's more, Eric's daughter resented all the ridicule of her dad by others and wondered, "What business is it of theirs?" Good question.

Your Choice—Lavish or Simple?

Pauline loves diamonds, the bigger the better. She also likes furs and fancy cars. Fortunately, she can afford these luxuries, but others think she's tacky. The wedding she and her husband planned for their daughter was lavish—truly extravagant, from the limos to the big orchestra. Many of the guests commented on the couple's bad taste—while they ate the wonderful food, drank the expensive wine, and danced to lively music until the wee hours.

Pauline had the time of her life and her husband gave her another diamond ring to add to her collection. Now the family is talking about that, too. Fortunately, Pauline doesn't give a hoot.

Alex has different ideas. He was raised in an household filled with crystal and gold. He had the best of everything and it was expected that he'd become a doctor, and perhaps even go into practice with his father and uncle. After his medical training was over, Alex joined a medical team that went to Latin America to treat people who didn't have ready access to medical care. After two years, he returned to his hometown and entered the family practice. So far, so good. However, his way of life was markedly different from that of his family. He lived in a second-hand camper, became a vegetarian, and even rode his bicycle to the office—in jeans and sneakers no less!

Alex is now close to forty and still living the same simplified lifestyle, although he and his wife and child now live in a modest house. Every year, he returns to Latin America to volunteer his services for a few weeks. His casual clothes and old car sometimes embarrass his parents, but he's created a way of life he feels good about. He considers himself an environmentalist and believes everyone will live more simply in the future. His wife has similar values and they quietly live out a lifestyle that, compared to the way Alex was raised, seems austere. But I know Alex, and like Pauline, he doesn't give a hoot.

If a new woman or man, or flashy possessions or a more simple way of life is what you want, by all means ignore the tongue-waggers and go for it. And keep in mind that when people criticize your choices, they will almost always claim that you haven't thought them out. If people don't like what you're doing, they could claim that you are "under a spell" (Eric's family), a "show-off" (Pauline's "friends"), or just plain "odd" (Alex's family).

Of course, there are many other explanations that could be used to criticize your choices. Depending on your particular choice, people could say that you are insecure (and therefore, vain), guilty about something (and therefore refuse to acquire certain things or dress a certain way), shallow (and therefore show off your possessions), afraid to die (and therefore go after a romance in mid-life), and on and on.

PERSONALITIES AND ACHIEVEMENTS

Self-image is not based solely on our looks and the material things we have or the kinds of friends we choose. We can also be dissatisfied with or proud of our mental attributes and accomplishments. And, without question, we judge others and ourselves based on stereotypes about what "smart" is, what "accomplished" is, and what we should and should not be interested in. I know women (and a few men, too) who would die before they'd admit to watching a soap opera. Yet we know that millions do or there wouldn't be so many of these shows. Some people hide the gossip magazine or tabloid they're reading if you run into them at the supermarket. People will brag about the prestigious schools their children or grandchildren go to, but say little about the grandson who's a janitor.

What we choose to disclose about ourselves and our families has much to do with the values we have adopted. For a week, listen to yourself and watch what you reveal and what you hide. You'll learn a lot about yourself by doing this. You can then decide if you care if others think you're stupid because you read romance novels. The important thing is, do you think you're stupid or are these novels a pleasurable way to escape for a few hours? If you don't talk about your grandchild who's having problems in school, you can examine the reasons for your silence. What or who are you competing with?

Perfect Lives, Perfect Lies

There will always be people who claim that everything is perfect all the time. These are the people whose children never gave them a second of worry, whose spouses are flawless, whose calendars are full, and whose grandchildren are geniuses. Most of us have met people like this, and if we come to know them well, we also find out they are liars. Unfortunately, from time to time we may base our decisions on the approval of these people who claim to have all the answers.

Ron is a successful dermatologist in an affluent town in the midwest. A few years ago he made a decision that turned out to be unwise—he married a snob. Becky would not allow Ron to live the way he wanted to, which was to continue spending time with his high school buddies. He liked to watch football and basketball and drink beer with these men, two of whom were truck drivers who lived close by. Becky restricted his association with these friends and forced Ron to go to concerts with her and attend fancy dinners. She never told anyone that he even had these friends, and to the outside world, they looked like the perfect couple. For a while, Ron went along with his wife to keep the peace—and because he thought she really did have his best interests at heart. After all, attending some of these events could help build his practice.

This marriage didn't make it, much to the surprise of those who knew the couple only by their public facade. After a couple of years of living Becky's way, Ron went back to his sports and beer. He was such a good doctor, and so well liked, that his practice flourished and he became quite comfortable financially. Becky, however, couldn't give up the image of the husband she wanted, and therefore, she couldn't stay with Ron. It was a amicable parting and fortunately, there were no children to consider.

We could say that these two people made a mistake. I suppose they did, but in the process of living together they also clarified what they want and need in life. Ron will not choose another social climber and Becky will face the fact that she needs a husband with a cultured image. Neither are bad people or losers. But what is right for one is wrong for the other.

I remember a lovely woman who simply was not as academically sharp as her younger sister or her older brother. Consequently, she lived life in their shadows. Her sister was an accomplished cellist who played in a famous orchestra, and her brother was a top physicist, while she was "merely" the mother of four children. Now in her fifties, she has never felt significant in any way. Nothing she does will ever measure up. Perhaps she believes she is the child her parents seldom mention.

Stories like this are common. But as individuals, we all have worth in many areas, and the happiest people I've known were those who appreciate their own unique skills and attributes. We should be the ones to determine what we strive for and whether what we do is good enough. If we don't take on the challenge of living by our own star, we run the risk of living out someone else's idea of right, not our own.

WHO'S CALLING WHO WEIRD?

When you make decisions intuitively, based on your internal sense of what is right for you, you may decide to save money for that plastic surgery or drop the whole idea. You might decide to sell your house and live on a boat or you may proudly wear your expensive fur coat to the grocery store. Someone, somewhere, will say you're crazy, wrong, tacky, odd, or weird.

Nate is a "free spirit." He doesn't work at a regular job and spends most of his time wandering around town talking to people or sitting in the park reading newspapers and books. He does odd jobs to support himself and lives in a rented room. Most people in town know him and many think he's slightly deranged. The rest just think he's weird.

Actually, Nate is neither. I've spoken to him many times and it's clear to me that he's made his own choice about how he spends his time. If he wanted to, he's capable of making a decision to live another way. Nate once told me that he though most of the people in the town were really nice, but he also said, "a lot of them are kind of weird."

Happiness is a complex concept, and it's also relative and rather illusive. No one can tell you how to be happy any more than other people can tell you what you need—try as they will. Your body image, your clothing and household furnishings, your hobbies and occupation may be components of your happiness. Just make sure that you are on your own side when you make these choices. Remember the old saying: "If I'm not for myself, who shall be for me?"

Nine

Moving Forward In Your Own Way

I strongly believe in the principles I've presented here and I try to live them myself. In my professional life as a counselor, I also try to help my clients gain confidence in their own decisions.

However, I recognize that making independent decisions, based on your own values and needs, is not always easy. It is particularly difficult when moving forward if your own way results in you being criticized or belittled. And, since few people handle criticism well, you may be tempted to slide back to the comfortable range of choices. (Having read this far you no doubt know that no matter what you do, people will pick it apart and give you all kinds of reasons why your choice won't work out.)

When we add the voices of authority and expertise to the already loud chorus of family and friends, we could end up with dozens of messages, each presenting a different direction. In these days of talks shows, we all know that there is only one right way to do everything—and that changes from day to day. So if you're confused, don't worry about it. Everyone else is too.

I believe that in many, if not most, situations we can use our own minds and hearts to come up with our own answers. We can listen to our gut instincts, consider all sides of the issue at hand,

and move forward, knowing that we've made the best choice we can right now.

Unfortunately, there is a prevailing myth that life only presents us with challenges we can handle—alone! When we think about this myth, we know it isn't true. From the beginning of time, human beings have asked for help, sought advice, and leaned on other people when the going gets rough. That's the beauty of being interdependent—we don't have to stand alone all the time. In fact, in serious and potentially devastating situations, people may be so traumatized that without help, they are unable to go on with life in a full and normal way.

Sometimes people seek help to affirm what they already know. In other words, I may already have a strong inclination to take an action (or not take one) in a particular situation, but I ask a friend or my husband or one of my children to talk with me about my decision. Each may offer a different perspective on the issue, and I leave with more information to use as I consider my final choice. However, these individuals, close as they are to me, never tell me what to do, because they know it's my issue to explore, not theirs.

When you ask someone to hear you out, be sure that they understand the spirit and thinking behind your approach. You don't want to be told what do; you want help in exploring your own thoughts and feelings.

If you decide to use a professional to help you, the same principle applies. Too often, I've seen counselors misuse their position of authority by telling clients what to do and how to do it. However, that's not their job. Their role is to help you discover what is right for you. Establishing a relationship with a professional therapist or counselor is a big step, so I offer the following guidelines to help you choose wisely:

Examine qualifications.

It goes without saying that there are good and bad highly qualified counselors. That's why impressive credentials alone do not mean that a particular counselor is suitable for you. However, there are professional associations and referral services that can assist you in choosing among the pool of those who have met professional education and training standards. And of course, any therapist should willingly discuss his or her training and degrees. If a person is secretive or defensive about this issue, then you already have good reason to doubt professional competency.

Discuss fees, method of treatment, and expectations of counseling.

Do not be timid about asking questions in the first session, or even before the first visit. Some people are intimidated by these authority figures and don't ask about their philosophy of treatment. Thus an unequal tone is set in the beginning, and when things don't go well, the client may still be afraid to question what is occurring. Remember, the agenda in counseling is fundamentally yours to create. You have expectations and the counselor needs to know what they are. If he or she can't work within those expectations, then perhaps the counselor/client relationship won't blossom.

You are entitled to seek help on a short-term basis, meaning you may not want or need to commit to a lengthy treatment process. Like many of the clients I mention in this book, you may want to explore one major decision, or solve a particular marriage or family problem. Given the number of people in our society who have been in counseling more than once, it should not come as a surprise that people often seek assistance on a short-term basis for a specific reason. However, some therapists don't like to work this way, so be open about your needs.

Payment schedules should also be discussed in the beginning. Are you paying for each session at the time of the appointment; are you being billed; will your insurance company reimburse you? You might also explore a sliding scale fee schedule based on income. Some therapists are agreeable to such an arrangement, but some are not. Money issues in counseling can become tricky, so be clear about what you expect and ask questions about what the therapist expects.

Challenge if necessary.

Explore the therapist's attitudes, especially in the area of "right" and "wrong" decisions. Does the therapist have a broad value system, or does he or she define correct and incorrect actions more narrowly? Do you sense that the therapist is judgmental in certain areas? While it is true that you and your therapist may have different values, the professional should not try to impose his or her values on you.

A therapist often offers advice, but that is not his or her primary function. Generally speaking, a therapist is there to support you in what you think and feel. In other words, if you find a counselor saying, "You shouldn't feel that way," or "Don't believe that," then you are not being helped to explore your own feelings and beliefs.

Good counselors help you understand why and how you came to think or feel a certain way about many issues in life and how your actions are influenced by your attitudes. Through this process of supporting you, a therapist can help you look at issues in a new way. The counselor can also help you gain the necessary confidence to make desired changes in your life. If you believe you are being undermined by the counselor as you make your changes and choices, then speak up. Some other problem could be getting in the way, and it might not be your issue.

After a few sessions, if you find yourself holding back information because the therapist seems judgmental or critical, discuss this immediately. If the issue can't be resolved and there are specific problems you can't freely discuss, then you probably will have reservations about continuing therapy. However, remember that some of the best therapeutic relationships develop after the conflicts and problems arising between the counselor and the client are openly aired and discussed. A good "fit" may not be immediately apparent and the working relationship must be developed along the way.

How This Works In Practice

Let's look at some examples in which a good counselor/client match may not work. If you are seeking marriage counseling, but you consider divorce an option, then find out if the counselor is willing to help you with separation and divorce issues—if that's what you ultimately decide to do. You could find that the counselor considers divorce a "failure," perhaps even his or her failure to help the marriage stay intact. Thus, this person might not be the appropriate counselor for you. You may need to find a person who offers a wider range of services, so to speak, and who does not have a hidden agenda that attempts to keep every marriage together, no matter what.

Moral issues may arise too. Perhaps you are having problems with your same-sex live-in lover. Will a therapist who believes that being gay is morally wrong be able to help you? Probably not. I've had clients who sought help for this very problem, and I learned that previous therapists spent much of their counseling hour trying to lead them away from their homosexuality. These therapists have a right to their own value system. However, clients who are satisfied and comfortable with their sexual orientation may find it impossible to work with this type of therapist.

Paul, an acquaintance of mine, ran into trouble with a therapist who believed that one should always honor one's parents. Paul's primary issue involved his desire to break off a relationship with his mother, who had been verbally and physically abusive to him all his life. Unfortunately, she would not admit that the behavior had taken place, and therefore, the process of amends and forgiveness could not be accomplished. Paul could no longer tolerate her behavior and made a decision to write her a letter stating why he was ending all contact. His therapist did not accept this as an emotionally healthy choice.

While many therapists believe, as I do, that in most cases, attempts should be made to maintain relationships with family members, this isn't always the best solution for a client. I have seen this again and again and have supported my clients when reconciliation attempts have failed. Paul's therapist was rigid in his belief, however, and ultimately, therapy was terminated because of this impasse. Paul knew in his own heart that he simply had to have at least a temporary "separation" from his mother. On his own, he worked out the best way to accomplish this. Fortunately, he had the support of his wife and one of his two siblings.

Therapists who support clients in unpopular and unconventional decisions are sometimes accused of being "yes" persons. This strikes me as another way to dismiss the idea that people can learn to stand alone and make good choices. Certainly, no therapist will sanction behavior that is clearly unacceptable. I wouldn't stand by idly if a client made a "decision" to physically hurt another person, continue a harmful addiction, or act in some other obviously reckless way.

While most therapists are not irresponsible and passive in the face of clearly destructive actions, a small number may be prone to wielding their power and taking advantage of a hurt, vulnerable client. Sometimes people are so needy that they will blindly follow the therapist's advice without considering it carefully. This is a sad situation, because the client has little opportunity to explore his or her own attitudes and feelings.

SMALL AND BIG DON'T MATTER

As I've tried to practice what I preach, I've learned that the principles apply to both large and small issues. In fact, some of the so-called little things make all the difference in the quality of our lives. For example, for many years I joined my family on the ski slopes, hating every minute of it, but not wanting to disrupt the family vacations by staying home. Besides, my loved ones persisted in telling me that skiing would help me stay in shape, so it clearly was "wrong" for me to quit. Some family members even believed that if I didn't join them, I'd be ruining their fun. Fun? What fun? I was cold and wet, and while they'd whiz past I was shaking in my boots, dawdling on the hill. When other skiers bumped me I was sure that this was the big fall I'd always feared. And the lift—every time I got on one I was convinced it was leading me to my doom. Am I clear? Skiing is torture for me.

After some years of this nonsense, I called it quits. Protests followed. But I told my family that my feelings were as important as theirs, and while I agreed to continue going to the ski resorts, the slopes and I would no more meet. Now I stay warm in the cabin with my big pile of books and magazines and meet up with the others at the end of the day. Odd as it seems, some members of my family are still disappointed that I don't share their enthusiasm for this sport, but they have come to respect my wishes. My only regret is that I didn't make this decision sooner.

As I examine my own actions in relation to this one small decision, I realize that it has always been easier for me to stand firm and make decisions based on my own gut feelings when I'm the only one involved. When others could be affected, then I often put their feelings ahead of my own. (That way, I could feel noble, or like a "good" wife, mother, whatever.) So I have had some experience in doing exactly what I've told others not to do. I kept on with the dreaded skiing, for example, because my family had subtly convinced me that they knew what was best for me. Their "concern" for my health and my physical fitness blinded me to the simple fact that there are lots of ways to exercise, and furthermore, it's none of their business how I choose to stay fit.

Writing this book is another fine example of the way some people have tried to convince me that they know what is best for me. Some friends and even a few colleagues told me that these ideas would be met with harsh criticism. After all, I'm saying that getting even with a person, having an affair, quitting careers and projects, and so forth just may be okay—or at least not always wrong. "This isn't what a therapist should say," I've been told again and again.

For some years, the negative and critical voices held me back. My ideas remained strong and I was committed to them, but I didn't look for a way to write and publish this book. Ultimately, I decided to follow my own advice and discuss the project with people I'd not approached before. Remember, I've suggested seeking positive support if those around you are negative. I needed to do that, too. I also decided to tell my family that I had made a firm commitment to pursue the project. Previously I'd only joked about it—a common ploy to avoid being taken seriously.

Once my family realized that I was truly serious, their attitude changed, too. Lo and behold, they began to get behind me and encourage me. Their message was, "go for it." My dear son-in-law, David, began planning how to sell this yet unwritten book in his store. A few therapist friends began to enthusiastically encourage my efforts, which helped me continue. When my coauthor, Virginia, who was more than positive, came into my life, we were able to bring this book into being by working together.

I share this to demonstrate how we can bring good things into our lives once we get behind ourselves. If we hang around negative people with their "it will never work," "you'll be criticized," "it's too ambitious a project" cautions, we invariably become stuck. But when we have the courage to make a commitment to ourselves and our desires and choices, others often join our bandwagon. I've seen this in my own life and in the lives of my clients.

INDEPENDENCE ISN'T NEW ANYWAY

As I've written this book, I've thought about the way many famous and respected people have been subjected to ridicule, criticism, and even more drastic consequences as they pursued their decisions. It was once conventional wisdom that the world was flat and it was okay for Africans to be owned as slaves. Popular opinion once held that women were not suited to the intellectual life and even voting would ruin their femininity.

Suffragists and abolitionists and modern day civil rights leaders were thrown in jail for acting on convictions that are now considered mainstream. And just think of all the people who did the "wrong" thing by hiding Jews or helping Jewish families escape Nazi persecution during the 1930s and 1940s. One can only wonder about the outcome of that most awful period in history if only more Germans had courageously followed their own ideas rather than remaining safe and conventional.

We can list one example after another that illustrate these large ethical issues and name the famous people who were involved. But ultimately, these issues come home. I've had clients whose anti-Vietnam War stance resulted in alienation from their families. I've known physicians and therapists who were ostracized by colleagues when they explored "holistic" healing methods. One client's family told her they wouldn't tolerate her "women's libber" talk at holiday dinners, and another was accused of being unpatriotic because he protested the recent Persian Gulf War.

Sometimes it's easier to see the wisdom of making firm, individual decisions when the issues are global and involve basic values. I mention these large issues because they clearly illustrate the desirability of going against the conventional and the popular. But bring the big principles down to the personal, and you'll easily see how they can work for you.

You may have been ridiculed or criticized in your family for espousing an unpopular cause. If so, then good for you. You've had experience and can apply it to every decision you make, even those that seem less important. But if a personal decision is going to change your life, then by definition it's important.

I hope you will come to realize that you have the ability to understand your own ideas, attitudes, opinions, and feelings better than anyone else, including all the authority figures in your life. Yes, respect their knowledge and ideas, but respect your own, too.

If you are reading this book while stuck in a painful situation and you need to move forward, I hope that you find a positive, supportive message here. And I hope you will understand that no matter how entrenched negative messages are, they can be uncovered and thrown away. You can defy authority and do what you believe is right.

SOME FINAL THOUGHTS

The answers to life's dilemmas can—and should—come from your heart. Furthermore, you usually know when you've made a choice that just doesn't feel right. Examine why you were compelled to make a decision that left you unsatisfied and unhappy. Did you listen to advice you knew wasn't good for you, but you feared not listening? Perhaps you believed you *must* listen because the weight of someone else's authority was behind the words. Remember, you alone will reap the benefits and pay the consequences for your choices. No matter what age you are, it's not too late to make sure your choices are really your own.

Use the following ideas to reinforce your resolve to make decisions in your own way. Consider this a review of the principles presented in this book, and use them as a guide anytime you're confused and wondering what the best choice might be.

Define your own priorities.

Others will always have ideas about what is right for you, usually based on their idea of what's right for them. To live a happier, more satisfying life, clarify your own values. What are your big dreams? What are the most important goals you want to accomplish? What do you need for your own happiness? Never live out another person's idea of what's right for you. Although many will try, no one can tell you what you need in life or what it takes for you to be happy.

Define your own attitudes.

We develop our attitudes based on influences from many different people and circumstances. No one is immune. We are all influenced by family, friends, religious authorities, experts in many fields, the media, our past experiences, and so on. It's easy to operate our lives from attitudes that really aren't our own, but rather ones that others have defined for us. Sure, it may be difficult to go against the conventional views and attitudes that surrounds you. But remember, you are the best judge of what's right and wrong for you.

Examine your feelings about love, marriage, and divorce.

As I said before, you may have many more choices than you think. You are the only person who can decide if you should get married or stay single, stay married or get a divorce, have children or stay childless. Moreover, you are entitled to structure your relationships to suit your needs and desires. We've never had so many options, many of them the result of giving up old, sometimes deeply ingrained, ideas about what is right and wrong. Likewise, you are equally entitled to live according to the values you were raised with; you don't have to change to accomodate shifting attitudes about relationships. Everyone, it seems, has advice to offer in this area. No wonder we're all confused sometimes. For this reason, always keep in mind that it's *your* life—and *your* relationships.

Examine your belief system about sexuality, fidelity, and infidelity.

It's possible that you may not always know what's right and wrong in these areas. Many of your ideas may have come from others who tried to tell you about the so-called right way to handle sexual issues. These people base their advice on *their* beliefs and value system, but there are many gray areas in this realm of life; no one has yet come up with one set of ideas that satisfies everyone. I believe it's wise for you to sort through the possible ideas and beliefs and come up with what is good for you. It's your right to challenge any ideas that just don't fit.

Decide how you want your relationships with parents, children, and siblings to work.

Relationships with family members can be about as complex and difficult as life gets. With so much "expert" advice around, it's easy to become overwhelmed. Furthermore, it's difficult to defy convention when it comes to family, the one institution many hold sacred. While I advise clients to work out satisfactory relationships with their families, I also know that it's sometimes impossible.

Working it out with family sometimes can mean coming up with an unconventional solution or even deciding not to resolve a problem. For example, perhaps you'll decide not to make peace with a family member, and you'll be roundly criticized for this choice. However, you're the one who will live with—or without—this relationship, so listen to your heart and do what you think is best.

Choose your own career and lifestyle.

If you sometimes believe that a particular lifestyle has been imposed on you, then once again, you may be living out someone else's idea of what is best for you. The same applies to your work and career. For example, you may have stayed in a stifling job simply because others convinced you that you have it made. Think carefully about this issue and make changes, even small ones, that will enable you to live in accordance with what you really want. When you truly appreciate your own unique skills and attributes, choices about your goals, style of dress, home, career, and interests will come more easily.

***Don't always strive for perfection
and be willing to make mistakes.***

Sometimes it's best just to get the job done and behind you. You're more likely to procrastinate if you think you must make every decision perfectly and carry out every action without error. This is impossible, anyway, so give up the ideal of perfection now. If and when you do make a mistake, remember that each choice you make, good or bad, teaches you something about your beliefs and values. Believe me, you *can* learn from your mistakes, and as I've said, most mistakes can be fixed.

Give up now and then.

So, you've started a fabulous needlepoint wall hanging, or at least it will be fabulous if you ever finish it. Too bad you hate needlepoint; too bad you were taught to never quit. But when you start making decisions in your own way, it's likely you'll take that hated project and throw it out, or donate it to a thrift shop, or maybe pass it on to a friend who would love to finish it. If you simply can't learn to love your new job, then maybe a change is in order; if, no matter what you do, you can't make a relationship work, then maybe it is time to give up trying; if you just don't like your new house, then perhaps you should admit you made a bad choice, put the house on the market, and move as soon as you can. Sometimes enough really is enough, and knowing when to give up can be one of your most important strengths.

Forget the rules—or at least change them.

Sometimes we live by rules as if they'd always been there, never questioning whether everyone in the world lives by the same set of guidelines. But just look at history. Thank goodness for all the people who dared to break "the rules." Trust your own intellect to determine which rules should be followed and which simply don't apply to you, confident in the knowledge that some of the most important people in history have done just that.

Lower your expectations.

You know the truth. Sometimes life is mundane, irritating, even boring. Once you accept this, you'll be happier with the rest of life—the highs, the excitement, the challenges. Much happiness comes from the mundane, however, and don't overlook the pleasure of sharing a cup of coffee with your best friend, the thrill of your grandchild's smile, the enjoyment of a good novel, or the view outside your window. If you associate happiness only with big achievements, landmark events, or those times when everything is going your way, you're bound to spend much of your life in a dissatisfied state. Remember, too, that it's okay to experience sadness, worry, unhappiness, and longing. Don't let anyone, no matter how authoritative they seem, tell you what you should feel, think, or believe. And last of all…

Follow your heart as well as your head.

That's what this book is all about. Some people will argue that this only leads to disaster, but in my experience, making decisions from your own heart and with your deepest wisdom—even if they are sometimes painful choices—is truly the most satisfying way to live. When you have the courage and the conviction to make your own choices, chances are, they will be the right ones—because you made them by yourself for yourself.

As you practice the principles in this book, you'll become more proficient at making wise choices. And don't forget to look for more positive influences in your life. Never let anyone tell you that your heart is defective in some way. You know better. New friends, a new environment, or professional counsel may be able to help you if you're having difficulty making decisions your way. So surround yourself with people who respect your right to live your own life, using your own best judgement.

It is my greatest hope that you have a happy, healthy, satisfying life. Believe firmly in your ability to create your own life in your own way, and it can happen.

About The Authors

Sylvia Bigelsen is a psychotherapist specializing in marriage, divorce, and family counseling. Originally a teacher, she received her master's degree from Fairleigh Dickenson University and her Ed.S. from Seton Hall. She has given numerous presentations on topics ranging from AIDS to coping with stress and anxiety. The mother of three grown children, she resides with her husband in New Jersey.

Virginia McCullough is the author or coauthor of numerous books, including *Testing and Your Child, Coping With Radiation Therapy,* and *TMJ: The Overlooked Diagnosis*. The mother of two children, she lives in Asheville, North Carolina.

Additional copies of *When The Wrong Thing Is Right* may be ordered by sending a check or money order for $9.95 to

>MasterMedia Limited
>17 East 89th Street
>New York, New York 10128

Or call (800) 334-8232 or fax (212) 546-7638. Please include $2 for postage and handling of the first copy, $1 for each additional copy.

MasterMedia's authors are available for speeches and seminars. Contact Tony Colao, speakers' bureau director, at (800) 453-2887 or fax (908) 359-1647.

OTHER MASTERMEDIA BOOKS

At bookstores, or call (800) 334-8232 to place a credit card order.

AGING PARENTS AND YOU: *A Complete Handbook to Help You Help Your Elders Maintain a Healthy, Productive, Independent Life,* by Eugenia Anderson-Ellis, is a complete guide to providing care to aging relatives. It features practical advice and resources for adults helping their elders lead productive lives. Revised and updated. ($9.95 paper)

BALANCING ACTS! *Juggling Love, Work, Family, and Recreation,* by Susan Schiffer Stautberg and Marcia L. Worthing, provides strategies to achieve a balanced life by reordering priorities and setting realistic goals. ($12.95 paper)

BEATING THE AGE GAME: *Redefining Retirement,* by Jack and Phoebe Ballard, debunks the myth that retirement means sitting out the rest of the game. The years between 55 and 80 can be your best, say the authors, who provide ample examples of people successfully using retirement to reinvent their lives. ($12.95 paper)

BEYOND SUCCESS: *How Volunteer Service Can Help You Begin Making a Life Instead of Just a Living,* by John J. Raynolds III and Eleanor Raynolds, C.B.E., is a unique how-to book targeted at business and professional people considering volunteer work, senior citizens who wish to fill leisure time meaningfully, and students trying out career options. ($9.95 paper, $19.95 cloth)

THE BIG APPLE BUSINESS AND PLEASURE GUIDE: 501 Ways To Work Smarter, Play Harder, and Live Better in New York City, by Muriel Siebert and Susan Kleinman, offers visitors and New Yorkers alike advice on how to do business in the city as well as how to enjoy its attractions. ($9.95 paper)

BREATHING SPACE: Living and Working at a Comfortable Pace in a Sped-Up Society, by Jeff Davidson, helps readers to handle information and activity overload, in order to gain greater control over their lives. ($10.95 paper)

CITIES OF OPPORTUNITY: Finding the Best Way to Work, Live, and Prosper in the 1990s and Beyond, by Dr. John Tepper Martin, explores the job and living options for the next decade and into the next century. This consumer guide and handbook, written by one of the world's experts on cities, selects and features forty-six American cities and metropolitan areas. ($13.95 paper, $24.95 cloth)

THE CONFIDENCE FACTOR: How Self-Esteem Can Change Your Life, by Dr. Judith Briles, is based on a nationwide survey of six thousand men and women. Briles explores why women so often feel a lack of self-confidence and have a poor opinion of themselves. She offers step-by-step advice on becoming the person you want to be. ($12.95 paper, $18.95 cloth)

CUPID, COUPLES & CONTRACTS: A Guide to Living Together, Prenuptial Agreements, and Divorce, by Lester Wallman, with Sharon McDonnell, is an insightful, consumer-oriented handbook that provides a comprehensive overview of family law, including prenuptial agreements, alimony, and father's rights. ($12.95 paper)

DARE TO CONFRONT! *How To Intervene When Someone You Care About Has a Drug or Alcohol Problem*, by Bob Wright and Deborah George Wright, shows the reader how to use the step-by-step methods of professional interventionists to motivate chemically dependent people to accept help they need. ($17.95 cloth)

THE DOLLARS AND SENSE OF DIVORCE: *The Financial Guide for Women*, by Dr. Judith Briles, is the first book to combine the legal hurdles by planning finances before, during, and after divorce. ($10.95 paper)

THE ENVIRONMENTAL GARDENER: *The Solution to Pollution for Lawns and Gardens*, by Laurence Sombke, focuses on what each of us can do to protect our endangered plant life. A practical source book and shopping guide. ($8.95 paper)

FINANCIAL SAVVY FOR WOMEN: *A Money Book for Women of All Ages*, by Dr. Judith Briles, divides a woman's monetary life span into six phases, discusses specific issues to be addressed at each stage, and demonstrates how to create a sound money plan. ($15.00 paper)

FLIGHT PLAN FOR LIVING: *The Art of Self-Encouragement*, by Patrick O'Dooley, is a life guide organized like a pilot's checklist, to ensure you'll be flying "clear on top" throughout your life. ($17.95 cloth)

GLORIOUS ROOTS: *Recipes for Healthy, Tasty Vegetables*, by Laurence Sombke, celebrates the taste, texture, and versatility of root vegetables. Contains recipes for appetizers, soups, stews, and baked, broiled, and stir-fried dishes—even desserts. ($12.95 paper)

HOT HEALTH-CARE CAREERS, by Margaret T. McNally, R.N., and Phyllis Schneider, provides readers everything they need to know about training for and getting jobs in a rewarding field where professionals are always in demand. ($10.95 paper)

HOW TO GET WHAT YOU WANT FROM ALMOST ANYBODY, by T. Scott Gross, shows how to get great service, negotiate better prices, and always get what you pay for. ($9.95 paper)

KIDS WHO MAKE A DIFFERENCE, by Joyce M. Roché and Marie Rodriguez, is an inspiring document of how today's toughest challenges are being met by teenagers and kids, whose courage and creativity enables them to find practical solutions! ($8.95 paper, with photos)

LIFE'S THIRD ACT: Taking Control of Your Mature Years, by Patricia Burnham, Ph.D., is a perceptive handbook for everyone who recognizes that planning is the key to enjoying your mature years. ($18.95 cloth)

LISTEN TO WIN: A Guide to Effective Listening, by Curt Bechler and Richard Weaver, Ph.D.s, is a powerful, people-oriented book that will help you learn to live with others, connect with them, get the best from them, and empower them. ($18.95 cloth)

THE LIVING HEART BRAND NAME SHOPPER'S GUIDE, by Michael E. DeBakey, M.D., Antonio M. Gotto, Jr., M.D., Lynne W. Scott, M.A., R.D./L.D., and John P. Foreyt, Ph.D., lists brand name products low in fat, saturated fatty acids, and cholesterol. Revised edition. ($14.95 paper)

THE LIVING HEART GUIDE TO EATING OUT, by Michael E. DeBakey, Antonio M. Gotto, Jr., and Lynne W. Scott, is an essential handbook for people who want to maintain a health-conscious diet when dining in all types of restaurants. ($9.95 paper)

THE LOYALTY FACTOR: Building Trust in Today's Workplace, by Carol Kinsey Goman, Ph.D., offers techniques for restoring commitment and loyalty in the workplace. ($9.95 paper)

MAKING YOUR DREAMS COME TRUE: A Plan For Easily Discovering and Achieving the Life You Want, by Marcia Wieder, introduces an easy, unique, and practical technique for defining, pursuing, and realizing your career and life interests. Filled with stories of real people and helpful exercises, plus a personal workbook. ($9.95 paper)

MANAGING IT ALL: Time-Saving Ideas for Career, Family, Relationships, and Self, by Beverly Benz Treuille and Susan Schiffer Stautberg, is written for women juggling careers and families. With interviews of more than two hundred career women (ranging from a TV anchorwoman to an investment banker), this book contains many humorous anecdotes on saving time and improving the quality of life. ($9.95 paper)

MANAGING YOUR CHILD'S DIABETES, by Robert Wood Johnson IV, Sale Johnson, Casey Johnson, and Susan Kleinman, brings help to families trying to understand diabetes and control its effects. ($10.95 paper)

MANAGING YOUR PSORIASIS, by Nicholas J. Lowe, M.D., is an innovative manual that couples scientific research and encouraging support, with an emphasis on how patients can take charge of their health. ($10.95 paper, $17.95 cloth)

MANN FOR ALL SEASONS: Wit and Wisdom from The Washington Post's *Judy Mann*, shows the columnist at her best as she writes about women, families, and the impact and politics of the women's revolution. ($9.95 paper, $19.95 cloth)

MIND YOUR OWN BUSINESS: *And Keep it in the Family*, by Marcy Syms, CEO of Syms Corp, is an effective guide for any organization facing the toughest step in managing a family business—making the transition to the new generation. ($12.95 paper, $18.95 cloth)

OFFICE BIOLOGY: *Why Tuesday Is the Most Productive Day and Other Relevant Facts for Survival in the Workplace*, by Edith Weiner and Arnold Brown, teaches how in the '90s and beyond we will be expected to work smarter, take better control of our health, adapt to advancing technology, and improve our lives in ways that are not too costly or resource-intensive. ($12.95 paper, $21.95 cloth)

ON TARGET: *Enhance Your Life and Advance Your Career*, by Jeri Sedlar and Rick Miners, is a neatly woven tapestry of insights on career and life issues gathered from audiences across the country. This feedback has been crystallized into a highly readable guide for exploring who you are and how to go about getting what you want. ($11.95 paper)

OUT THE ORGANIZATION: *New Career Opportunities for the 1990s*, by Robert and Madeleine Swain, is written for the millions of Americans whose jobs are no longer safe, whose companies are not loyal, and who face futures of uncertainty. Provides advice on finding a new job or starting your own business. Revised. ($12.95 paper, $17.95 cloth)

THE OUTDOOR WOMAN: *A Handbook to Adventure*, by Patricia Hubbard and Stan Wass, details the lives of adventurous women and offers their ideas on how you can incorporate exciting outdoor experiences into your life. ($14.95 paper)

PAIN RELIEF: *How to Say No to Acute and Chronic Pain*, by Dr. Jane Cowles, offers a step-by-step plan for assessing pain and communicating it to your doctor, and explains the importance of having a pain plan before undergoing any medical or surgical treatment; includes "The Pain Patient's Bill of Rights," and a reusable pain assessment chart. ($22.95 paper)

POSITIVELY OUTRAGEOUS SERVICE: New and Easy Ways To Win Customers for Life, by T. Scott Gross, identifies what '90s consumers really want and how business can develop effective marketing strategies to answer those needs. ($14.95 paper)

POSITIVELY OUTRAGEOUS SERVICE AND SHOWMANSHIP, by T. Scott Gross, reveals the secrets of adding personality to any product or service and offers a wealth of nontraditional marketing techniques employed by top showpeople, from car dealers to restaurateurs, amusement park operators to evangelists. ($12.95 paper)

THE PREGNANCY AND MOTHERHOOD DIARY: Planning the First Year of Your Second Career, by Susan Schiffer Stautberg, is the only undated appointment diary that shows how to manage pregnancy and career. ($12.95 spiralbound)

REAL BEAUTY...REAL WOMEN: A Handbook for Making the Best of Your Own Good Looks, by Kathleen Walas, International Beauty and Fashion Director of Avon Products, Inc., offers expert advice on beauty and fashion for women of all ages and ethnic backgrounds. ($19.95 paper)

REAL LIFE 101: The Graduate's Guide To Survival, by Susan Kleinman, supplies welcome advice to those facing "real life" for the first time, focusing on work, money, health, and how to deal with freedom and responsibility. Revised. ($9.95 paper)

ROSEY GRIER'S ALL-AMERICAN HEROES: *Multicultural Success Stories*, by Roosevelt "Rosey" Grier, is a candid collection of profiles of prominent African Americans, Latins, Asians, and Native Americans who revealed how they achieved public acclaim and personal success. ($9.95 paper, with photos)

SELLING YOURSELF: *How To Be the Competent, Confident Person You Really Are!* by Kathy Thebo and Joyce Newman, is an inspirational primer for anyone seeking to project a positive image. Drawing on experience, their own and others', these entrepreneurs offer simple techniques that can add up to big successes. ($11.95 paper)

SHOCKWAVES: *The Global Impact of Sexual Harassment*, by Susan L. Webb, examines the problem of sexual harassment today in every kind of workplace around the world. Practical and well-researched, this manual provides the most recent information available, including legal changes in progress. ($11.95 paper, $19.95 cloth)

SIDE-BY-SIDE STRATEGIES: *How Two-Career Couples Can Thrive in the '90s*, by Jane Hershey Cuozzo and S. Diane Graham, describes how to learn the difference between competing with a spouse and become a supportive power partner. Published in hardcover as *Power Partners*. ($10.95 paper, $19.95 cloth)

THE SOLUTION TO POLLUTION: *101 Things You Can Do To Clean Up Your Environment*, by Laurence Sombke, offers step-by-step techniques on how to conserve more energy, start a recycling center, choose a biodegradable product, and even proceed with individual clean-up projects. ($7.95 paper)

THE SOLUTION TO POLLUTION IN THE WORKPLACE, by Laurence Sombke, Terry M. Robertson, and Elliot M. Kaplan, offers everything employees need to know about cleaning up their workplace, including recycling, using energy efficiently, conserving water, and buying nontoxic supplies. ($9.95 paper)

SOMEONE ELSE'S SON, by Alan A. Winter, explores the parent-child bond in a contemporary novel of lost identities, family secrets, and relationships gone awry. Eighteen years after bringing their first son home from the hospital, Trish and Brad Hunter discover they are not his biological parents. ($18.95 cloth)

STEP FORWARD: Sexual Harassment in the Workplace, by Susan L. Webb, presents the facts for dealing with sexual harassment on the job. ($9.95 paper)

THE STEPPARENT CHALLENGE: A Primer For Making It Work, by Stephen J. Williams, Ph.D., offers insight into the many aspects of step relationships—from financial issues to lifestyle changes to differences in race or religion that affect the whole family. ($13.95 paper)

STRAIGHT TALK ON WOMEN'S HEALTH: How to Get the Health Care You Deserve, by Janice Teal, Ph.D., and Phyllis Schneider, is destined to become a health-care "bible." Devoid of confusing medical jargon, it offers a wealth of resources, including contact lists of healthlines and women's medical centers. ($14.95 paper)

TAKING CONTROL OF YOUR LIFE: The Secrets of Successful Enterprising Women, by Gail Blanke and Kathleen Walas, is based on the authors' professional experience with Avon Products' Women of Enterprise Awards, given each year to outstanding female entrepreneurs; offers a plan to help you gain control over your life, plus business tips as well as beauty and lifestyle information. ($17.95 cloth)

TEAMBUILT: Making Teamwork Work, by Mark Sanborn, teaches businesses how to increase productivity, without increasing resources or expenses, by building teamwork among employees. ($12.95 paper, $19.95 cloth)

A TEEN'S GUIDE TO BUSINESS: The Secrets to a Successful Enterprise, by Linda Menzies, Oren S. Jenkins, and Rick R. Fisher, provides solid information about starting your own business or working for one. ($7.95 paper)

TWENTYSOMETHING: Managing & Motivating Today's New Work Force, by Lawrence J. Bradford, Ph.D., and Claire Raines, M.A., examines the work orientation of the younger generation and offers managers practical advice for understanding and supervising their young employees. ($12.95 paper, $22.95 cloth)

WHAT KIDS LIKE TO DO, by Edward Stautberg, Gail Wubbenhorst, Atiya Easterling, and Phyllis Schneider, is a handy guide for parents, grandparents, and baby sitters. Written by kids for kids, this is an easy-to-read, generously illustrated primer for teaching families how to make every day more fun. ($7.95 paper)